See How
SHE LOVES US

See How
SHE LOVES US

Fifty Approved Apparitions of Our Lady

JOAN CARROLL CRUZ

> *Mary has made herself all to all, and opens her merciful heart to all, that all may receive of her fullness; the sick, health; those in affliction, comfort; the sinner, pardon; and God, glory.*
> —St. Bernard (1090–1153)

TAN Books
An Imprint of Saint Benedict Press, LLC
Charlotte, North Carolina

Nihil Obstat: Msgr. Gerald Lefebvre
                  Censor Deputatus

Imprimatur: ✠ Very Rev. Than N. Vu, S.T.L., V.G.
                  Vicar General
                  Baton Rouge
                  February 3, 2011

ISBN: 978-0-89555-718-6

Cover design by Milo Persic, milo.persic@gmail.com.

Cover image: Mary of the Rosary of San Nicolas.

Printed and Bound in the United States of America.

TAN Books
An Imprint of Saint Benedict Press, LLC
Charlotte, North Carolina
2012

Dedicated to the loving memory of my son,
Michael David Cruz,
who lived quietly, suffered patiently,
and died peacefully
in the embrace of the Church.

CONTENTS

ACKNOWLEDGMENTS

AM deeply indebted to all the people at the shrines who so graciously answered my queries and in addition sent pictures, booklets and books. I appreciate their help, their generosity and kindness. I note especially the following:

Very Reverend Father A. Michael, Rector of the Shrine Basilica of Our Lady of Health, Vailankanni, India; Frère Basile of the Sanctuaire Pellevoisin, France; Père Yves-Marie Couet, Director of the Shrine of L'Île Bouchard, France; Philippe Lecourtier of La Salette, France; Secrétaire General, Tanguy Lafforgue, Sanctuaire de Nôtre-Dame de Laus; James J. Marsala, Shrine of Our Lady of Good Help, Green Bay, Wisconsin; M. Rene Fantin, Nôtre-Dame-de-l'Osier, France; Piegni Dilibri, Shrine of Our Lady of Mercy, Savona, Italy; Antoni Ravier, Santa Maria de Guadalupe, Guadalupe, Spain; Père Pierre de Couessin, Recteur du Sanctuaire Marial Diocesan, Querrien, France; Mr. Claude Lacroix, Nôtre-Dame de Garaison; Administrator Sanktuarium Matki Bozej Lichenskiej, Poland; Administrator S. Andrea Delle Fratte, Roma; Antonio Rodriguez Rodriguez, Santuario Ntra Sra de Chandavila, La Codosera, Spain; Angelika Kuhn of the shrine in Marienfried, Germany; Administrator of the Pontifico Santuario in Pompeii; Jairo M. Rodriguez of the Shrine of Our Lady of Cuapa, Nicaragua; Jean-Clause Bauchat of the Shrine of Our Lady of La Salette, France; Pierrot di Geronimo, Shrine of Our Lady of Banneux, Belgium; The Santuario San Nicolas, Argentina; Abbé Jean-Pierre Herman, Chapelain aux Sanctuaires de Beauraing, Belgium; Secretary of the Shrine of Nôtre-Dame of Pontmain, France; Lea Fantin, Representative of the Shrine of Nôtre-Dame-de-l'Osier, France; Don Rocco Di Filippo of Castelpetroso; the Brothers of the Immaculate of Castelpetroso; Dr. Rainer Killich, Kevelaer, Germany; Frère Jean-Marc,CSsR, Nôtre-Dame des Trois-Epis; Rev. Joseph Kung of the Cardinal Kung Foundation; Paulette Crutzen and Pierrot Di Geronimo of the Sanctuaire de Banneux; Sanktuarium Matki Bozej Lichen-skiej; Fr. Roland D. Mactal, O.P. for the Images of Our Lady of Manaoag, Philippines; Fr. Carlo M. Rossato of Monte Berico; Marian Therese Horvat, Ph.D. of www.TraditionInAction.org; Msgr. Gerald Lefebvre and Father Than N. Vu of the Diocese of Baton Rouge; Rosalie Turton of the 101 Foundation; Pat Lavelle of Our Lady of Knock Shrine; P. Carlo M. Rossato of Santa Maria di Monte Berico; M. Kleemann, Pfarrsekretarin of the shrine Muttergottes von Heede; Adolfo Alvarez of the shrine of Nuestra Senora de Ocotlán; Ms. Amber Backus of the shrine of Our Lady of Good Help; and Hong Duong of the Shrine of Our Lady of La Vang.

AUTHOR'S NOTE

APPARITIONS of the Blessed Mother have occurred during all ages of the Church beginning in AD 39 when tradition tells us that she appeared to St. James the Great in Zaragoza, Spain. Many lists exist that detail apparitions from that time, some of which have been regarded as trustworthy according to the local church authorities. However, it is uncertain when the Church first established rules by which to judge the authenticity of these occurrences.

Only a few of the many hundreds of reported visions have been recognized by the Vatican. These private revelations have been judged by the Church to be credible and worthy of belief, though they do not belong to the deposit of faith.* The visions reported in this book have either earned the approval of the Vatican or the approval of the local bishop who acted under the directives given by the Vatican, and the Congregation for the Doctrine of the Faith. The last directive concerning this matter was approved by Pope Paul VI on February 24, 1978, which gives the local bishop the primary responsibility to judge an apparition's authenticity. If the bishop considers the event genuine, he may then give permission for processions and all expressions of faith.

In a few of the accounts in this book, approval for expressions of faith has been granted, though the investigation of the apparition is still under way.

Even before directives of the Congregation of the Doctrine

* (*Catechism of the Catholic Church*, 67, http://www.vatican.va/archive/ENG0015/__PH.HTM)

of the Faith were given, and before the regulations of Pope Paul VI, bishops had the authority to approve an apparition without formally declaring the supernatural origin of it. They either declared the apparition to be genuine or implied their approval by permitting churches to be built as requested by the vision, and by consecrating the churches in elaborate ceremonies. They assisted at the burial of many visionaries and permitted statues and images of the vision to be crafted, and blessed and crowned these images. Many popes have also conveyed their belief in the apparitions by visiting the apparition sites and have blessed and crowned statues representing the vision. Many have also issued documents in observance of anniversaries relating to the apparitions.

Since the diocesan bishop's main concern is upholding the faith of his people, he is very cautious before offering a decision. In almost all cases the bishop will organize a committee to help in determining if the vision is authentic. The committee will consider if the apparition has a supernatural element and if the individuals under consideration are mentally balanced, honest, and sincere, and if they participate in the sacraments. The committee will judge if the apparition is free from theological errors and that the message of the vision does not try to correct or add anything to the doctrines of the Faith, but instead contributes to a deeper understanding of the Faith. The bishop may allow expressions of faith at the site of the apparition even while the committee is deliberating or gathering evidence.

For the purpose of this book we have decided to begin by relating the details of the vision that took place in Aylesford, England, in 1251, which the Church accepts fully. There are Church-approved visions that followed that apparition, which occurred throughout the world until modern times when the Blessed Mother appeared in Egypt in 2009.

With the exception of three visionaries in this book, two being nuns and one a banker, as well as the saintly visionaries of

Our Lady of Mount Carmel, all the other apparitions were witnessed by humble folk, shepherds, simple village people, many children and mostly uneducated people. Their sincerity, religious dedication, local respectability, mental balance and obedience to Church authorities have been carefully considered.

The apparitions in this book have the added blessing that they have produced the conversion of millions, the construction of some of the largest Roman Catholic churches in the world, the creation of Marian Movements and Societies, the spread of Marian devotions, especially the Rosary, and the increased participation in many Marian pilgrimages.

As attested to by these apparitions, our Heavenly Mother has come down to earth to heal, console, instruct, advise, encourage, warn against diseases and physical dangers, to protect against plagues, famines, droughts and for many other reasons. Our Lady has also left us healing springs of water as a memorial.

Her many visitations have proved her care and motherly concern for us. After reading about the visions in this book, you will no doubt agree with me and give a heartfelt sigh in declaring with gratitude and pleasure, "See how she loves us!"

—Joan Carroll Cruz

See How
SHE LOVES US

OUR LADY OF MOUNT CARMEL

Aylesford, England, and Avignon, France
1251 and Fourteenth century

BEGINNING AND GROWTH OF THE CARMELITE ORDER

ISTORY reports that the great Prophet Elias, before the birth of Christ, ascended the holy mountain of Mount Carmel in Palestine and began a life of prayer and contemplation that was to inspire the beginning and growth of the Carmelite Order. Sometime after the Prophet Elias was taken up into Heaven as related in Scripture's Book of Kings, several men, inspired by the prophet, took up residence in the caves of Mount Carmel to live as hermits. After the Incarnation, their successors erected on the Mount the first chapel ever dedicated to the Mother of God.

Because of the invasion of infidels and due to the increase in vocations, many men ventured into Europe while some were being invited to do so. St. Louis IX, king of France, invited the hermits to settle in France. Because of these migrations, it became necessary to change some of the rules. The hermits were then forced to become mendicants who depended on the generosity of the people for their necessities. This presented serious difficulties for the religious Orders already established who resented the newcomers and their needs and responded with various types of harassment.

ST. SIMON STOCK APPEALS TO OUR LADY OF MOUNT CARMEL

History then reports that St. Simon Stock, who had left England for the Holy Land, returned to his native land when the Muslims invaded. On his return to England, he joined the Carmelite Order and was eventually elected prior. He appealed to the patroness of the Order, Our Lady of Mount Carmel, on July 16, 1251, with this prayer that is still recited frequently by members of the Order:

> Flower of Carmel,
> Blossoming vine,
> Splendor of Heaven,
> Mother Divine,
> None like to thee,
> Peerless and fair,
> Thy children of Carmel,
> Save by thy care,
> Star of the Sea.

Suddenly a great flood of light filled his cell. In the company of many angels, the Blessed Virgin, with the Child Jesus, presented the brown scapular to him with this promise: "This shall be the privilege for you and for all Carmelites that whoever dies piously wearing this scapular, shall not suffer eternal flames."

The scapular had already been worn at times as a protective garment during work and consisted of two lengths of fabric joined at the shoulders so that the scapular lies front and back. With the recognition given by the Queen of Heaven, the scapular became a permanent and much respected addition to the Carmelite habit. After the apparition and after numerous appeals for protection against the Order's antagonists, Pope Innocent IV on January 13, 1252, sent a letter of protection that secured the Order from the problems they encountered.

Some years later, when St. Peter Thomas (1305–1366) was engaged with important missions of the papal court, Our Lady of Mount Carmel again favored her Order. Concerned about the Order, he heard these words: "Have confidence, Peter, for the Carmelite Order will last until the end of the world. Elijah, its founder, obtained it a long time ago from my Son." It was during this fourteenth century that many, attracted to the Carmelite Order and the many privileges it enjoys, became members of the Order by way of confraternities. They then participated in the graces, benefits and observances of the Order, and were properly enrolled in the Confraternity or Third Order.

THE SABBATINE PRIVILEGE

Another vision took place, this time to Pope John XXII on March 3, 1322. Now known as the Sabbatine Privilege, Our Lady revealed: "I, the Mother of Grace, shall descend into Purgatory on the Saturday after their death and whomsoever I shall find in Purgatory I shall free." St. Robert Bellarmine explains the promise to mean, "that anyone dying in Mary's family will receive from Her, at the hour of death, either the grace of perseverance in the state of grace or the grace of final contrition."

On learning of this vision, Pope Benedict XV encouraged all to wear this "common armor . . . which enjoys the singular privilege of protection even after death."

Sixteen popes have given their approval to this Privilege, including Pope Paul V who issued a decree on its behalf. Many saints have also added their approval. The Carmelite Order, for various reasons, no longer speaks of it. Nevertheless, the faithful members may still believe in this extraordinary promise based on their faith in the mercy of our heavenly parents.

POPE PIUS XI SPEAKS FOR THE SABBATINE PRIVILEGE

Six hundred years after the vision of Pope John XXII in which the Sabbatine Privilege was revealed, Pope Pius XI observed the occasion by writing in 1922:

> It surely ought to be sufficient to merely exhort all the members of the confraternities and third orders to persevere in the holy exercises which have been prescribed for the gaining of the indulgences to which they are entitled and particularly for the gaining of the indulgence which is the principal and the greatest of them all, namely, that called the Sabbatine.

Many saints have spoken highly of the scapular, including St. Alphonsus Liguori and St. Claude de la Colombière who announced: "I aver without a moment's hesitation that the Scapular is the most favored of all." It is regarded as the most indulgenced of all sacramentals.

BERNADETTE WORE THE SCAPULAR AS DID POPE JOHN PAUL II

It is claimed that Bernadette always wore the scapular and had one of her apparitions on the Feast of Our Lady of Mount Carmel. At Fatima, too, Our Lady of Mount Carmel appeared during the spectacular miracle of the sun. Our Lady of Mount Carmel also appeared at Castelpetroso, Italy, during a vision that was witnessed by many. It is also of interest to realize that the scapulars of St. Alphonsus and St. John Bosco were found intact during their exhumations and are still preserved in reliquaries. Additionally, Blessed Pope John Paul II joined the

Discalced Third Order of Mount Carmel as a young man and always wore the scapular, even when in the hospital after the attempt on his life.

Our Lady of Guadalupe

Caceres (Guadalupe), Spain
1326

THE people of Caceres (Guadalupe), Spain, experienced great emotion when a cowherd named Gil Cordero related that a radiant Lady emerged from a nearby forest while he was searching for a lost cow. The Lady then indicated where he should dig to find a treasure and requested that a chapel be built in commemoration of her visit.

When Gil Cordero convinced authorities to visit the place, they found the entrance to an underground cave, which contained a statue that had been hidden for six hundred years, according to the documents that were also unearthed. The documents revealed that the statue had been presented in the year 580 by St. Gregory the Great to the noted churchman, Bishop Leander of Seville. During the frightful time of the Moorish invasion in 711, the statue was hidden for safekeeping. Those who had secured the statue evidently died during the conquest and it was thus lost for centuries.

Although hidden for so long a time, the statue, made of oriental, unstained wood, was examined and pronounced to be in perfect condition. The simple structure that was first constructed long ago was replaced later by a chapel that was built by order of King Alfonso XI. The church, and the statue enthroned therein were named "Guadalupe," for the village near the place of discovery.

In 1340, the king of Spain went with great pomp and majesty to visit the miraculous statue, fourteen years after the statue's discovery. Many noblewomen also visited and prayed before the statue and provided costly garments to adorn Our Blessed Mother. In fact, so many garments were provided that a special room called the Reliquary Cabinet was provided for their exposition. Among these articles of interest is a luxurious head-dress, worn on special occasions, which contains countless gems donated by Our Lady's devotees.

The statue, which is very dark, is regarded as a symbol of Our Lady's royal maternity because she holds in her left hand the Divine Child and in the right hand a royal scepter.

It is recorded that Columbus carried a replica of the statue with him, as also did the Conquistadors. Christopher Columbus is also known to have prayed at the shrine before making his historic voyage and that, upon discovering the West Indies Island of Karukera on November 4, 1493, renamed it Guadalupe in honor of the Blessed Mother.

The miraculous statue is reverently enshrined in a room called the Camarin at the fortress-like monastery of Guadalupe, located behind the main altar. The place befits the Mother of God who sits on a modern enamelwork throne fashioned in 1953.

The holy influence of this miraculous statue reached across the Atlantic Ocean to Mexico in the year 1531, where Juan Diego experienced apparitions of Our Lady. The miraculous portrait of Our Lady on fragile cloth that appeared as a result of Juan Diego's apparitions was first given the Aztec name *Te Quatlasupe*. This means one who crushes the head of the stone serpent. Bishop Juan de Zumarraga, who was from Spain and was familiar with the shrine of Our Lady of Guadalupe in Caceres, Spain, mistook the Aztec name *Te Quatlasupe* to be Guadalupe. Thereafter, the miraculous portrait of Our Lady in Mexico has shared the name Guadalupe with the faraway image in Spain.

MADONNA OF MOUNT BERICO

Vicenza, Italy
1426 and 1428

THE Sanctuary of Mount Berico is located high above the city of Vicenza and provides a sweeping view of distant valleys, cities, farmlands, and the majestic Alps. Because of its location, the sanctuary serves as a veritable lighthouse for the region. It was here that Our Lady deigned to visit on two occasions to console and provide help during the stressful times of the plague.

According to manuscripts of the time, from the year 1404 until after the year 1428, the territory was shaken and tormented by pestilence and sickness, so much so that the population declined drastically both from the many deaths due to sickness and those who were fleeing it.

In those trying years, a seventy-year-old woman of Vicenza, Vincenza Passini, went up the hill each morning to bring food to her husband who worked in his small vineyard. Documents reveal that Vincenza led a simple and honest life and was devoted to her faith, and especially nurtured a heartfelt devotion to the Mother of God. She attended church services regularly and was mindful of the poor.

THE FIRST VISION

At nine on the morning of March 7, 1426, Vincenza was climbing to the top of the hill as was her custom, when she saw in front of her a woman who, according to documents, was "in the likeness of a most beautiful queen, with garments more resplendent than the sun, wreathed in a fragrance of a thousand scents." Vincenza was so overcome by the beauty of the vision that she swooned and fell to the ground.

When she recovered, the Blessed Virgin identified herself,

> I am the Virgin Mary, the Mother of Christ who died on the Cross for the salvation of men. I beg you to go and say in my name to the people of Vicenza that they must build in this place a church in my honor if they want to recover their health, otherwise the plague will not cease.

Weeping with joy and kneeling in front of the Madonna, Vincenza questioned, "But people will not believe me. And where, O glorious Mother, will we find the money to do these things?"

The Madonna replied,

> You will insist so that my people do my will, otherwise they will never be rid of the plague and until they obey, they will see my Son angry with them. As proof of what I say, let them dig here and from the rock living water will spring and, as soon as the building begins, money will not lack.

After saying this, the Madonna, with a graceful movement took a twig, traced the Sign of the Cross on the ground and even drew the shape of the church to be built. She then planted the twig in the ground where the high altar of the shrine now stands.

The Lady then added,

> All those who visit this church with devotion on
> my feast days and on every first Sunday of the
> month, will be given an abundance of grace and
> the mercy of God and the blessing of my motherly
> hands.

Vincenza immediately obeyed the vision and began telling everyone she met, but she soon realized no one believed her. The plague had forced people to think about other matters. She then went to Bishop Pietro Emiliani, who also gave little value to her report. In the meantime, the plague raged on. Vincenza resumed her work and her deeds of charity and on feast days she climbed the hill to pray on the spot where the Madonna had stood.

THE SECOND VISION

According to other documents, the Virgin once again appeared to Vincenza, this time on August 1, 1428. The Lady repeated her previous warning and her recommendation for the health of the people. Because of the horrific plague conditions, the people then believed her and had a change of heart. The severity of the plague had induced the people to seek help from the Madonna. The council and the Hall of Government decided to build the church on Mount Berico and began work only twenty-four days after the last apparition. As soon as the church was completed, the plague disappeared and from that day, the region no longer suffered from it.

The Lady had spoken of water that would spring from a rock at the place where the shrine was to be built. While the earth was being dug for the shrine, "a wonderful and incredible quantity of water welled out like a spring . . . overflowing like an abundant river that ran down the hill with great noise."

A beautiful statue of the Madonna of Mount Berico is

enthroned in the shrine, now a grand basilica, to receive the prayers and veneration of her people. Documents in the archives describe the statue as being, "An imperious image in marble, painted with skill in various and precious colors." It depicts the Madonna with an open smile. Her head is framed by curls, and she wears a gold-decorated veil, a gold-colored dress with a greenish, gold-edged mantle. Figures of children, women and men are huddled beneath the mantle that drapes over the Virgin's extended arms. The Blessed Mother also wears necklaces and a golden crown that was placed there by Cardinal Giuseppe Sarto, the Patriarch of Venice, who was the future Pope Pius X.

THE THIRD VISION

During the First World War, the city of Vicenza was behind the lines of conflict. Thoroughly frightened, the people made a solemn vow to the Madonna of Mount Berico promising that if they and their lands remained safe, they would observe the birthday of the Madonna every year in a special way. The Madonna answered the prayer of the people so that every year, on September 8, great crowds of people visit the sanctuary to offer their gratitude. Because of the many people who visit on that day, plus those who observe the Madonna's wishes that they visit her on the first Sunday of every month, it became necessary in 1972, to construct next to the basilica two large chapels with both upper and lower levels. Also constructed were thirty additional confessionals inside the basilica.

The Servants of Mary took possession of the shrine in the year 1435, and have been ministering to the pilgrims ever since—almost six hundred years.

VISITS BY POPES

In addition to Pope Pius X who crowned the Madonna, the basilica has been honored by the visit of Pope Paul VI, who announced on January 11, 1978,

> We decree that the Most Blessed Virgin Mary be honored with the name of Madonna of Mount Berico and that from now on truly be the principal patron next to God of the city and diocese of Vicenza.

In observance of the centenary of the crowning of the image, Pope John Paul II sent a message to the Patriarch of Venice, Cardinal Marco Ce, from Castel Gandolfo on August 22, 2000, in which he recounted his visit to the Madonna stating,

> I too had the joy of making a pilgrimage to the Shrine of Mount Berico on 7–8 September 1991 to ask the Blessed Virgin to bless the people of the area and to show herself to be the tender and provident Mother of those who suffer and those who long for justice and peace.

OUR LADY OF THE GUARD

Ceranesi, Mount Figogna (Genoa), Italy
1490

*L*OCATED in the municipality of Ceranesi, Mount Figogna lies in the northwestern part of Italy, a little north of Genoa. Known as the boyhood home of Christopher Columbus, Genoa is also renowned as the home of St. Catherine of Genoa whose incorrupt body lies in the church dedicated to her memory. The area is also celebrated as the place where the miraculous image known as Our Lady of the Guard is reverently enshrined.

THE FIRST VISION

Atop the tall mountain known as Monte Figogna are numerous church buildings whose history involves a peasant named Benedict Pareto. He was grazing his flock on the mountain when his attention was drawn to a brilliant movement. Within this heavenly glow was a woman holding a child on her arm. As the lady approached him, Benedict Pareto felt compelled to kneel.

Standing before him, the beautiful Lady assured him, "Do not be afraid. I am the Queen of Heaven and have come to you with my Divine Son for this reason. You are to arrange for a church to be built on this spot, to be dedicated in my name."

When the poor man protested that he had no money with which to build a church the Lady calmed his confusion with the words, "Trust me, Benedict. The money will not be lacking; only your own good will is needed. With my aid all will be easy."

After the Lady departed, and after Benedict recovered from the sweetness and beauty of the apparition, he felt a great urgency to report the event to his parish priest and ran excitedly down the mountain path. The priest and Benedict's neighbors, on hearing about the event, were skeptical.

THE SECOND VISION

Sometime later, when Benedict climbed a fig tree looking for fruit, he fell and broke a number of bones. We are told that he was carried to his home where he received the Last Sacraments. Because he was unable to move, he deeply regretted that he could not share Our Lady's request with those in a position to provide what she wanted. While he grieved, the Blessed Mother once more appeared to him and again requested a shrine at the place of her first appearance. When the Lady left, Benedict Pareto was instantly cured.

His neighbors, who knew the severity of his injuries and his immediate cure, replaced their skepticism with wholehearted belief. They again listened to Benedict's story of the apparition and, with the authorization of the parish priest, they contributed to a fund for the building of a small oratory on Mount Figogna. That oratory was constructed and later replaced in 1530, by a large chapel that was maintained by a group of laypeople and members of Benedict's family, including two of his sons.

Following the Council of Trent, the Bishop of Navarra visited the sanctuary in 1582 to enforce regulations formulated by the Council. After learning about the history of the shrine, he formally rendered his approval and looked favorably upon an artistic relief located on the high altar, which depicts the scene of the first apparition.

On May 27, 1604, the history of the shrine was again approved, this time by the Archdiocese of Genoa. The papers drawn as a result of an inquiry were duly notarized and can still be found in the Genoa State Archives. As a result of this study, permission for the publication of miracles was given and devotion to Our Lady of the Guard was authorized.

MIRACLE OF OUR LADY OF THE GUARD, 1625

Of all the miracles attributed to Our Lady of the Guard, the most famous is that which took place in 1625, when Charles Emmanuel, Duke of Savoy, marched on Genoa with an army of fourteen thousand men. Knowing they were outnumbered, a saintly Capuchin lay brother, Fra Tomaso da Trebbiano, exhorted the people to pray to Our Lady of the Guard for protection. The next day, when the Duke attacked, he was roundly defeated by a small band of peasants who had been sent into battle with the blessing of their parish priest. The victory was everywhere accepted as a miracle of Our Lady of the Guard.

During the second half of the nineteenth century, a new shrine was built to accommodate the huge increase in the number of pilgrims. A hospice was erected, as well as a guesthouse.

There are three statues named for Our Lady of the Guard. After the victory at Genoa, a marble statue was placed in a chapel on the mountain which marks the actual site of the first apparition. The second statue is found in the wayside chapel of St. Pantaleon on the mountainside. The third statue is found above the high altar in the church on Monte Figogna. This statue was given a formal coronation in 1894, as commanded by Pope Leo XIII. This wooden statue depicting Our Lady was credited with numerous miracles which are confirmed by costly tokens of appreciation given to the shrine and by thousands of ex-votos which decorate the walls of the church.

The shrine has been recognized by many popes who granted special indulgences to the devotees, including Pope Clement XVI, Pius VI and Pius XII. One native son of Genoa, who had a particular devotion to Our Lady of the Guard, was elevated to the Chair of St. Peter as Pope Benedict XV. It was this pope who assigned to the church the title of Basilica on March 11, 1915.

Two additional popes who honored the shrine were Pope John Paul II who visited on September 22, 1985, and the reigning Pope Benedict XVI who prayed there on May 18, 2008.

OUR LADY OF TROIS-EPIS
(OUR LADY OF THE THREE EARS)

Orbey, France
1491

THE FIRST VISION

A BLACKSMITH by the name of Thierry Schoeré who lived in the village of Orbey, was on his way to market on May 3, 1491 when he stopped by an oak tree. A man had died there of a fatal accident and in his memory his family had placed a crucifix on the tree near where he fell. Thierry got off his horse and knelt down to say a prayer for the repose of the victim's soul. Suddenly Thierry was dazzled by a bright light and in it he distinguished the Blessed Mother dressed in a long white veil. She was holding three ears of corn in her right hand while the other hand held a clump of ice. Without identifying herself she began to speak,

> Arise, brave man. See these ears? These are the symbols of fine harvests that will reward virtuous and generous people and bring peace and contentment in the homes of faithful Christians. As to the ice, it means hail, frost, flood, famine and all its attendant misery and desolation that will punish disbelievers with the gravity of their sins which tire the Divine Mercy. Go down to the village and

announce to all the people the meaning of these prophecies.

When the vision disappeared, the blacksmith became terribly frightened, and on reaching the village, he said nothing, in disobedience of the Lady's wishes. He went inside the market, purchased a sack of wheat and started to adjust it on the back of his mount. But the sack of wheat became uncommonly heavy and could not be lifted. Even with the help of others, the sack could not be moved. It was then that he remembered the words of the Virgin, and realizing that the weight of the sack was a signal to him, he loudly shared the message that had been entrusted to him. Many people heard the message spoken with sincerity and took it to heart, resolving to do better in the future. When he had finished telling of his experience and the message given to him, he easily lifted the sack of wheat, secured it on his mount, and left for home.

CHAPEL IS BUILT ON THE APPARITION SITE

During the summer of the same year, a wooden chapel was built on the site of the apparition. Pilgrims made their way there and miracles were reported. Eventually, this little church was enlarged with the addition of other buildings. For many years, various religious Orders conducted services for the many pilgrims who came from all parts of the country, especially on May 3, the anniversary of the apparition.

For the 519th anniversary in 2010, special services were held. During this observance, many ears of corn were blessed by several priests. These priests, the Redemptorists, have cared for the shrine since 1911.

Four years following the apparition, in 1495, after careful investigations were conducted, the suffragan* of Basel authorized worship† at the shrine, and all demonstrations of faith.

---

* The relationship expressed between a bishop and his archbishop. As suffragan, a bishop yields precedence of honor, even in his own diocese, to his archbishop. But in the government of his diocese a bishop is independent of archiepiscopal jurisdiction. Along with other suffragans, a bishop has equal votes in provincial councils, held under the presidency of the archbishop. (From Fr. Hardon's *Modern Catholic Dictionary*), http://www.catholicculture.org/culture/library/dictionary/index .cfm?id=36695, accessed 3/19/2012.

† "Worship" as applied to Our Lady does not mean "adoration." It means "honor" in this context.

Our Lady of Garaison

Monléon-Magnoac, France
1515

THE FIRST VISION TO ANGLEZE SAGAZAN

HE history of the chapel begins with a ten-year-old shepherdess, Angleze Sagazan, who was with her flock near the source of the River Cier in the Pyrenees of southwestern France. The Blessed Mother favored the simple child by appearing to her on three different occasions.

Our Heavenly Mother, wanting to relieve the hunger and distress of the people, asked for a chapel to be built in her honor, "Where I will spread my gifts."

Angleze dutifully told her father what took place after the first vision, but was met with skepticism by him and the people who first heard the story. Some of the people nevertheless accompanied Angleze to the spot where the vision occurred in the hope of also seeing the Blessed Virgin, yet only Angleze was favored with the two following apparitions. Soon people from other areas journeyed to the place on pilgrimage, chanting hymns in honor of the Blessed Mother.

THE FOLLOWING TWO VISIONS CONVINCE
THE DOUBTERS

An historian of the time, Molinier, reports that the failure of crops was prevalent in the region so that the people were reduced to eating "a kind of bread, a pastry of mestain black." A painting in the heavily decorated chapel shows the visionary in the presence of Our Lady, holding a piece of this black bread which was miraculously changed to white. Another painting depicts a chest in the house of the Sagazan family full of fluffy white loaves being inspected by neighbors. The miracle that this painting represents is said to have convinced the people of the authenticity of the visions.

When cures were being obtained, and the devotion of the people increased to a sizable amount, the first simple chapel was enlarged in 1540, to accommodate them. The Virgin Mary's request was realized by this enlargement, and Angleze, no doubt filled with graces and virtues and the love of the Blessed Mother, left the beloved place of her encounters with Heaven and became a Cistercian nun at Fabas where she died in 1582.

The magnificent vaulted sanctuary that remains is a veritable treasury of art which dates to the late sixteenth and seventeenth centuries. Paintings, sculptures, gilded frames and altarpieces, bas-reliefs and intricate carvings are deemed most precious by the people and are greatly revered and admired by all who are fortunate to view them.

THE STATUE OF OUR LADY OF GARAISON
(A PIETÀ)

The statue of Our Lady of Garaison, which draws the attention of all, is a pietà dated from the sixteenth century. According to a painting on the wall of the chapel, the wooden statue is depicted as being thrown into a fire by the Huguenot captain, a Mr. de Sus. The statue was retrieved unharmed and is still enthroned above the main altar.

Of all the cures that have taken place at the shrine, the most notable one is that which was performed in the seventeenth century in favor of the young Louis XIV who had been brought there by his mother, Ann of Austria.

During the French Revolution of 1789, pilgrimages were interrupted, but were later re-established. A school was eventually built and all went well until the new anti-clerical laws of 1903. It was then that the school was closed, but twenty years later the school was re-opened, and today about 580 pupils are counted. The Baroque sanctuary is now surrounded by the school, the rectory, and necessary parish buildings, some of which accommodate visiting pilgrims.

The apparitions were recognized by two popes, Urban VIII and Gregory XVI who granted indulgences to those who visit the shrine, which was so blessed by the Mother of God.

Our Lady of Guadalupe

Mexico City, Mexico
1531

THE FIRST VISION

𝖂HEN Juan Diego, a fifty-five-year-old Indian who lived five miles north of Mexico City, was hurrying on Tepeyac Hill to attend Mass at a Franciscan mission, he heard a great many birds singing. Then, when they stopped, he heard a woman's voice calling him, not by his name, but by the affectionate diminutive, "Juanito, Juan Dieguito." She then asked, "Juan, smallest and dearest of my little children, where were you going?" After he explained that he was on his way to attend Holy Mass, the Lady said:

> Know for certain, dearest of my sons, that I am the perfect and perpetual Virgin Mary, Mother of the True God, through whom everything lives, the Lord of all things, who is Master of Heaven and Earth. I ardently desire a temple be built here for me where I will show and offer all my love, my compassion, my help and my protection to the people. I am your merciful Mother, the Mother of all who live united in this land, and of all mankind, of all those who love me, of those who cry to me, of those who have confidence in me. Here I will hear their weeping and their sorrows, and will remedy and alleviate their

sufferings, necessities and misfortunes. Therefore, in order to realize my intentions, go to the house of the bishop of Mexico City and tell him that I sent you and that it is my desire to have a temple built here. Tell him all that you have seen and heard. Be assured that I shall be very grateful and will reward you for doing diligently what I have asked of you. Now that you have heard my words, my son, go and do everything as best as you can.

THE SECOND VISION

When the bishop showed little interest in Juan's story of the apparition, Juan Diego returned to the hill and found the vision waiting for him. Pleading with her that she should send someone more worthy to deliver her message, he was told, "Listen, little son. There are many I could send. But you are the one I have chosen for this task. Tomorrow morning, go back to the bishop. Tell him it is the ever holy Virgin Mary, Mother of God who sends you, and repeat to him my great desire for a church in this place." Once again Juan visited the bishop who again dismissed him politely.

THE THIRD VISION

Juan Diego had already visited the bishop twice, but then, during the third visit, since Juan Diego seemed sincere and honest, the bishop asked for a sign from the Lady. This Juan duly reported to the Lady during her third apparition.

This fourth and final vision of Juan Diego took place on December 12 when Juan was hurrying to fetch a priest for his dying uncle. Suddenly the Lady appeared and asked where he was going. To his troubled explanation, the Lady spoke these consoling words:

> Listen and let it penetrate your heart, my dear little son. Do not be troubled or weighed down with grief. Do not fear any illness or vexation, anxiety or pain. Am I not here who am your Mother? Are you not under my shadow and protection? Am I not your fountain of life? Are you not in the folds of my mantle? In the crossing of my arms? Is there anything else you need? Do not let the illness of your uncle worry you because he is not going to die of his sickness. At this very moment he is cured.

The Lady then asked Juan to walk higher up the hill and collect the roses found there—this in spite of the rocky nature of the place, its unsuitability for the growth of any type of vegetation, and the December weather that was hostile to the development of roses. Nevertheless, Juan found a number of roses which he gathered in the scoop of his tilma, a cloak made of cactus fibers that was worn by the Indians. The Lady arranged the flowers and cautioned him against disturbing or revealing his burden except in the presence of the bishop.

When Juan opened his cloak for the prelate, he found not the usual rejection and skepticism he had received before, but the bishop kneeling among the flowers, looking in reverential awe at a picture miraculously applied to the cloak—an exact likeness that Juan Diego identified as the Lady he had seen four times on Tepeyac Hill.

When Juan Diego returned home after this miracle, his uncle related how the Lady had appeared to him and had restored him to perfect health. (This was actually the fifth appearance of Our Lady of Guadalupe.)

Because of the clamor of the people to pray before the image, the bishop had the cloak installed above the altar of the cathedral. Later it was placed above the altar of the church that was built according to the Lady's request.

Juan Diego lived seventeen years following the apparition. During that time he was appointed as the official custodian of the cloak and was ever ready to relate the apparitions and to answer all questions. He lived in a small room attached to the church and died at the age of seventy-four in the year 1548. He was beatified by Blessed Pope John Paul II during his visit to Mexico on May 6, 1990, and was canonized during another visit to Mexico by Pope John Paul II on July 31, 2002.

THE TILMA

The tilma itself is cactus cloth made from the maguey plant that usually disintegrates within twenty years and is a fabric similar to loose sacking. During its many examinations, it has been observed that the weave is so loose that if one stands behind it, the features of the basilica can be seen as clearly as through a trellis. The garment is made of three strips, each one measuring twenty-one inches in width by seventy-eight inches in length, with the image imprinted on two of the strips. In its golden frame, the third panel, which hung on Juan's back, is folded behind the two front panels. The two panels are joined with the original loose stitching that can be seen running the length of the panel along the left ear of the figure, down the left wrist to the knee and passing to the side of the angel's head. The figure of Our Lady measures four feet, eight inches in height.

Artists confirm that the tilma is a fabric wholly unsuited to the application of paint. They have reported that the portrait was painted without brush strokes, but like a wash in four different media: oil, tempera, water color and fresco. The application of these paints was so permanent that, compared to man-made paintings dating from 1531, the image has required no restoration and remains to this day an artistic marvel.

In 1666, 135 years after the apparition, a Painter's Commission was formed to study the miraculous portrait. During the same year a Scientific Board also examined it and praised it as being the work of God "Who alone is able to produce miraculous effects above all the forces of nature."

In addition, a University of Florida biophysicist examined the portrait in 1979 and declared that ". . . the painting is miraculous."

Through the years, additions were made to the cloak. The gilding, the silver added to the moon, and other embellishments have flaked or faded away while the original features have remained the same.

A discovery was made in 1929, when the eyes of the portrait were examined. Reportedly, a bearded face is seen in them, a shoulder, and part of a halo in a three-quarter image. This likeness matches exactly the contemporary portraits of Juan Diego. The finding was confirmed in 1951, and again in 1956, by renowned and respected oculists.

The natives who first studied the image read messages that were not apparent to others. Since the Lady stood in front of the sun, they understood that she was greater than their sun god Huitzilopochtli. Their moon god, Tezcatlipoca, likewise lost stature since the Lady stood upon the moon's crescent. The brooch at her throat with its small black cross reminded the Indians of the crucifixes of the Spanish friars and the symbol on the banner of Captain Hernando Cortes. That she was held aloft by a child with wings signaled her as a heavenly being, yet her hands joined in prayer meant that there was one who was greater. The white fur at the neck and sleeves was taken as a mark of royalty as were the forty-six golden stars and the border of gold. The bluish-green of the mantle was taken as a color reserved to divinity. It was the reading of the picture that converted whole tribes to the Faith.

Of the forty-five popes who have reigned since the creation of the miraculous portrait, twenty-five have issued decrees concerning it. The first was Pope Gregory XIII, dated 1575. Indulgences were granted by other pontiffs, including Pope Benedict XIV in 1754 who wrote:

> In the image everything is miraculous, an image emanating from flowers gathered on completely barren soil on which only prickly shrubs can grow . . . an image in no manner deteriorated, neither in her supreme loveliness nor in its sparkling color . . . God has not done likewise to any other nation.

Three popes have ordered the crowning of the image, and Pope John Paul II visited Mexico on five occasions, the first taking place in January 1979. On each of his visits, he prayed before the 450-year-old image of Our Lady.

The miraculous portrait continues to intrigue its viewers, puzzle artists, and baffle scientists.

OUR LADY OF MERCY

Savona, Italy
1536

THE FIRST APPARITION APPEARING TO
ANTONIO BOTTA

THE sumptuously decorated church of Savona owes its origin to an elderly farmer named Antonio Botta who witnessed the apparition of the Queen of Heaven on March 18, 1536. The farmer described the Virgin Mary as being dressed in white and surrounded by a dazzling light. The vision stood on a large rock overlooking a stream near the river Letimbro. As he knelt reverently before the vision, the Blessed Virgin directed Antonio to his confessor with the request that three Saturdays of fasting be observed and that three processions be organized in honor of God and the Mother of Jesus. The apparition then asked the farmer to return to the same place on the fourth Saturday to receive another message meant for the Curia and the people of Savona.

Obeying the words of the Madonna, Antonio went immediately to inform the local priest, Monsignor Bartholomew Zabreri, who then shared the message with the bishop of the diocese. Although they were receptive to the requests of the Madonna based on the sincerity and humility of the farmer, the mayor of the area, Genoese Doria, was not. He promptly summoned the farmer to the castle for questioning about the circumstances of the vision. Legend tells that during Antonio's interrogation, some fishermen off the coast of Savona saw three flames that rose high into the sky above the cathedral and the castle.

THE SECOND APPARITION

The second apparition took place on April 8, 1536, four Saturdays after the first visit of the Lady. She appeared with the same illumination and on the exact place of the first visit. The farmer recalled that she stood with outstretched hands extending downward in a gesture of mercy. Once again the Lady asked the elderly farmer for the three Saturdays of fasting and the processions, and praised the local fraternities and brotherhoods for their dissemination of the Word of God. She exhorted Antonio and his countrymen to follow the creed and disappeared with the words, "Mercy my son, not justice."

News of the apparition spread quickly and with such an increase in the number of pilgrims that a committee was formed to organize the influx. The large sums of money offered by the pilgrims resulted in the building of a place of worship. A chapel at the site of the apparition was soon authorized by Bishop Bartholomew Chiabrers on April 21, 1536. This new project was also approved by the city council of Savona, and Cardinal Spinola Horace, on July 24. By August 11 of that same year, the construction of the new church was begun.

Four years after the first apparition, the local community of Savona decreed that March 18 would be observed as an annual festival with a votive procession to the shrine.

SAVONA'S HOSPITALITY TO POPE PIUS VII

Savona is known for offering hospitality to Pope Pius VII who was exiled there by order of Napoleon in the year 1809, and held there until 1812. During those years he vowed that if he were released he would crown the statue of Our Lady of Mercy. The promise was kept when the pope placed a royal diadem on the statue on May 10, 1815.

More recently, the church and Our Lady were honored by the papal visit of Pope Benedict XVI who went there in pilgrimage on May 17, 2008.

OUR LADY OF OCOTLÁN

Tlaxcala, Mexico
1541

JUST ten years after the spectacular apparition of the Blessed Mother to Juan Diego in Mexico City, during which he received the Heaven-sent picture known as Our Lady of Guadalupe, another Juan Diego was thrust into history. His last name was Bernardino and he lived during a time when Tlaxcala, once the most populous and largest city in the country, was suffering an epidemic of smallpox. Estimates claim that nine out of ten Indians died as a result of the infection.

VIRGIN APPEARS TO JUAN BERNARDINO

To help Juan's relatives who had been stricken with the disease in the village of Xiloxostla, Juan walked to the River Zahuapan to collect water thought to have medicinal properties. After filling his jug with water, he made his way to the village through a thick grove of ocote trees. He abruptly halted at the sight of a beautiful woman of regal bearing standing among the trees. The reassuring smile of the Lady gave him the courage to draw closer to her. With a heavenly voice she greeted him: "May God preserve you, my son. Where are you going?"

Overcome by the woman's beauty and surprised at seeing her among the trees, Juan hesitated before he was able to reply,

"I am taking water from the river to my sick ones who are dying."

"Come with me," the Lady said, "and I will give you water to cure the disease. It will cure not only your family, but all who drink of it. My heart is ever ready to help those who are ill, for I cannot bear to see their misfortune."

Anxious to obtain miraculous water that would cure his relatives, Juan followed the lady with happy anticipation. When they came to a depression in the ground, the lady indicated a spring of fresh water.

In her soft, almost musical voice, she told Juan, "Take as much of this water as you wish and know that those who are touched by even the smallest drop will obtain, not merely relief from their illness, but perfect health."

Juan emptied his jug of the river water and filled it with the clear water of the spring. Wanting to express his gratitude, he turned to the Lady who then entrusted him with a message for the Franciscans at the Monastery of San Lorenzo where Juan was employed.

> Tell the religious for me that in this place they will
> find my image. It will not only manifest my perfec-
> tions, but through it I shall generously bestow favors
> and kindness. When they find the image they are to
> place it in the chapel of San Lorenzo.

When the Lady disappeared among the trees, Juan hurried to the village with his precious water. Upon reaching the bedside of his afflicted relatives, he told them about the Lady and the miraculous spring, as well as her promise of health through use of the water. Juan watched in amazement as the Lady's word was realized when each was restored to health after drinking the miraculous water.

FRIARS VISIT THE PLACE OF THE VISION

The next day Juan returned to the monastery and told the friars of his experience. After questioning him during the day, they decided that his story had merit and planned on visiting the place with Juan at night so as to avoid the curious.

Before reaching the place, they noticed a glow in the distance and when they arrived, the grove of ocote trees was afire. The largest tree in the grove, and this one alone, was burning along its entire length. Since nothing could be done, they left, but planned on returning after Holy Mass the next morning. With some of the parishioners, they set out and found a puzzling situation. The fire had destroyed only the lower branches of the surrounding trees—the tallest one, which had burned its entire length, was indeed blackened. Why the dry summer heat had not destroyed the other trees in a similar manner remained a mystery.

One of the friars had fortunately brought an ax with him and was instructed by the abbot to chop down the trunk of the large tree. A Mexican writer of the time left this report:

> A new marvel met their eyes: Within the trunk of the
> fallen tree was visible the image of the Holy Mother
> of God, representing the mystery of her Immaculate
> Conception—which can be seen today in the temple
> lovingly erected later by her children . . .

In this manner, the tale of Juan Diego Bernardino was fully verified in the presence of many witnesses. They agreed that the apparition of the Virgin Mary to her servant Juan Diego was a happy reality on the day she showed him the medicinal water and sent him to advise the religious where they would find her sacred image.

In a grand procession, and with the singing of hymns, the statue was brought to the chapel. There the abbot removed the statue of San Lorenzo and positioned in its place the miraculous image of the Mother of God.

We are told that the Indian sacristan resented the removal of the statue of San Lorenzo and placed the Lady's statue in another location during the night. The next morning the statue was found on the altar where it had been placed by the abbot. On at least two other occasions, the same marvel was repeated so that the sacristan became convinced of Our Lady's wish to remain where she had requested to be during the apparition. The 58-inch statue is now found in a magnificent niche or Camarin above and behind the altar of the Basilica of the Virgin of Ocotlán.

From the earliest days the statue was called Nuestra Senora de Ocotlatia which means Our Lady of the Burning Ocote. It is now simply called Our Lady of Ocotlán, Ocotlán being the Nahuatl word for "place of the pine tree." The beautiful statue of Our Lady is always dressed in costly vestments and wears a splendid golden crown which is surrounded by a halo of stars. The crown represents Our Lady's pontifical coronation in the year 1906.

DISTINGUISHED VISITORS TO THE SHRINE

Among the persons of distinction who visited the miraculous statue was the Archbishop of Puebla, Juan de Palafox y Mendoza, who visited it in 1644, and Archbishop Diego de Osoria de Escobar, who honored the Lady in 1670.

Additionally, the shrine of Our Lady was recognized by Pope Clement XII who authorized a feast day for Our Lady of Ocotlán and Benedict XIV who raised the shrine to the status of a basilica and granted indulgences and Apostolic indults to the faithful who venerate the image. Other popes also recognized the apparition, including Pius VI, Pius X and Pius XII.

One of the most beautiful churches in Mexico enshrines the statue of Our Lady of Ocotlán. Of interest to pilgrims, in addition to a visit to Our Lady, is the place of the miraculous spring and the small chapel that stands in the ancient ocote grove where Our Lady appeared to Juan Diego Bernardino.

Our Lady of Montallegro

Rapallo, Italy
1557

THE magnificent Sanctuary of Our Lady of Montallegro is nestled on a wooded hill, called the "Hill of Joy," overlooking the city of Rapallo. It was here that the Blessed Mother deigned to leave a precious icon depicting her dormition as she passed from this world to the Heavenly Kingdom. Our Mother is pictured lying on a bier with the Holy Trinity represented by the figures in the central part of the icon. Surrounding her in mournful attitude are several saints and two angels.

THE FIRST VISION

The discovery of the icon on the hill was made by a farmer, Giovanni Chichizola, on July 2, while he was walking nearby on a donkey trail. Suddenly he had an apparition of Our Lady who reassured him:

> Do not fear, Giovanni, I am the Mother of God. I have chosen you to be a messenger of my motherly will. Visit the ecclesiastics of Rapallo and let them know that the Mother of God has chosen this place as her perpetual dwelling place and would like

a church to be erected here. I leave here a pledge of
my love.

When the Virgin disappeared, the farmer discovered an icon
on a rock and attempted to remove it, but could not. He notified the villagers of Rapallo who journeyed to the hill, lifted it
and brought it to the church in Rapallo. The next morning the
icon had disappeared, only to be found where John had originally discovered it. Much to their surprise, a spring had started
to flow at the very place above which the Blessed Mother stood
during the apparition.

The villagers, once again, brought the icon to the church
where it was displayed all day to the veneration of many who
were impressed with the details of Giovanni's experience. In the
evening, the icon was locked away for safekeeping. They were
surprised the next morning when they discovered that it had disappeared once again., The icon was subsequently found on the
rock up the hill. All agreed that the mysterious travels of the icon
indicated the Blessed Mother's wish that it remain in that particular place, to be protected by the church she had requested.

CHURCH IS BUILT IN 1558

The very next year, 1558, the Archbishop of Turin authorized the building of a church on the Hill of Joy, which began
immediately. The following year it was opened and dedicated to
the Blessed Mother.

For seventeen quiet years the precious icon was loved and
venerated on the Hill of Joy until a group of Greek sailors, sail-
ing from Ragusa, experienced a storm while crossing the Gulf
of Tigullio. The ship's captain, Nicholas de Allegretis, together
with the crew, promised Our Lady that if they were saved, they
would make a pilgrimage to the nearest sanctuary dedicated to

her. Upon safely reaching land, they climbed to the sanctuary to fulfill their vow of thanksgiving. It was then that they noticed the precious icon and declared that it was formerly venerated in Ragusa, and that it had mysteriously disappeared from there in 1557. They claimed ownership, which resulted in court proceedings before the magistrate of Genoa. Eventually, the icon was given over to them for safe delivery to its former location.

The icon was taken to the port, boarded on the ship, and placed in a secure location. The ship was well out to sea when they found that it had disappeared. Eventually the captain and his crew learned that the icon had been discovered in the church where all agreed it was meant to stay.

APPARITION DAY

Every year on the anniversary of "Apparition Day," the people of Rapallo travel to the hill in a grand procession, carrying an ancient wooden crucifix and a silver shrine with the Mother's statue. Upon reaching the sanctuary, the first-time pilgrim is amazed by the huge collection of votive offerings and ex-votos, some of them in silver, which decorate the walls, giving proof of prayers answered and miracles worked through the Virgin's intercession. In the chapel of St. Joseph can be found the spring that began flowing from the time of the apparition. It is said to originate from the rock where the icon was originally found.

The pilgrim has two unique ways to reach the sanctuary on the Hill of Joy: by walking along an ancient mule track or by cable car from Rapallo, which was specifically constructed for the convenience of the pilgrims. The pilgrims are well rewarded when reaching the sanctuary. They are intrigued with its beauty and can pray before the miraculous icon of Our Lady of Montallegro.

Joining in the celebration for the 450th anniversary of the

apparition of Our Lady of Montallegro, in 2007, was Tarcisio Cardinal Bertone, the Secretary of State of the Vatican. The feast day of Our Lady is celebrated with great joy on the first three days of July.

Our Lady of Good Health

Vailankanni, India
1580

THE FIRST APPARITION AT VAILANKANNI

*L*OCATED on the shore of the Bay of Bengal, on the east coast of India, the magnificent church dedicated to Our Mother of Good Health came into being because of three apparitions. The first involves a young boy who was on his way to sell milk in a nearby village, but who stopped to rest under a banyan tree near a large pond. Suddenly Our Lady appeared to him, holding a beautiful baby. She asked the boy if she might have some of the milk for Her Son. After giving her some of the milk, he proceeded to his customer's home and apologized for being late and for not having the full amount of milk that had been expected. Yet, the pot of milk was full. After telling the Hindu man about the appearance of the Lady, the man followed the boy to the place of the apparition. When they reached the pond, the Lady appeared once again. When news of the apparition reached the ears of the Catholic community they were ecstatic and dedicated the place, naming it Our Lady's Pond. Thereafter, they journeyed there in procession to submit their prayers to the Lady who had graciously visited them.

THE SECOND APPARITION

The second apparition took place at the pond where a crippled boy sat on the shore selling buttermilk. Once again the Blessed Mother and Child appeared and once again she asked for some milk for her Child. He gave her some without hesitation. Then the apparition asked the boy to tell of the vision to a certain wealthy Catholic man in the nearby village. The boy jumped up and ran to fulfill the Lady's request, not realizing at first that his leg had been cured. The man who had been named by the Lady had had a vision the previous night in which Our Lady asked him to build a chapel for her. Together the man and the once-crippled boy returned to the site of the miracle. The Lady appeared to both of them and, soon after, a small chapel was built in honor of the Mother of Good Health.

THE THIRD APPARITION

The third apparition took place a few years later when wealthy Portuguese merchants experienced a violent storm at sea that wrecked their ship. Imploring the help of the Blessed Virgin, they safely reached the shore of Vailankanni and were taken to the chapel to give thanks to the Mother of Good Health. In gratitude for their miraculous rescue, they built a permanent chapel which was dedicated on September 8, the feast of the Nativity of Mary and the date of their safe return.

FESTIVALS, PILGRIMAGES, AND MIRACLES

Presently, an annual festival lasting nine days draws more than a million pilgrims, many of whom are of different faiths and languages. The large number of pilgrimages is likened to

Lourdes which also receives countless devotees of Our Lady.

As time passed, the many cures and answers to prayers at the shrine necessitated a larger one. Through the years, the shrine developed with numerous enlargements and additions into the magnificent church that stands today. Above the main altar is a statue depicting the Mother of Good Health, a popular attraction.

Numerous priests have ministered at the shrine and succeeding bishops and archbishops have approved the tradition, consecrated the various chapels that replaced former chapels, and granted numerous indulgences for all who worshiped there.

An Apostolic brief of Pope John XXIII, dated 1962, elevated the Shrine of Vailankanni to a minor basilica.

OUR LADY OF SILUVA

Siluva, Lithuania
1608

HE land was very sandy and barren in this region, making it difficult for the poor farmers to provide for their families who were staunchly Catholic and especially devoted to the Blessed Mother. The Catholic religion prevailed until the Protestant Reformation in the mid-sixteenth century swept through Europe. Lutheranism then flourished and Calvinism soon followed. Not even the little village of Siluva was spared. In 1532, the Calvinist influence was so great that the governor of the little village converted to it, as did the nobility and intellectuals throughout the country. A result of this Calvinist influence was the suppression of the Faith and the confiscation of Church property. Schools were given to Calvinist propaganda, while religious gatherings were prohibited. The poor people were not only enduring the hardships inflicted on them under the Calvinists, but were also suffering the loss of their churches.

When the Siluva church was about to be closed, the parish priest, Fr. John Holubka, obtained an ironclad box and placed in it liturgical vestments, chalices, and documents which proved that the property had been given to the church by Vytautas the Great. The most carefully placed item was a painting of the Blessed Virgin holding the Child Jesus that had been given to the church in 1457, and had been prominently positioned above the

51

main altar. The box was sealed and buried deep in the ground near a large rock. The priest's actions seemed inspired because a short time later, the authorities seized the church for their Calvinist activities. Eighty years went by with only the elderly being true to the Faith. But then the Blessed Mother intervened.

THE FIRST APPARITION AT SILUVA

It was summertime in the year 1608, while children were tending their flocks in a field on the outskirts of the village. They were gleefully playing and singing songs when they suddenly stopped, and beheld a beautiful young woman standing on a large rock, holding a beautiful baby in her arms. The children's happiness soon turned to deep sadness when they saw the woman weeping bitterly. The apparition did not speak, but looked heartbroken, with tears running down her cheeks and splashing on the rock.

The children described the apparition as glowing with light. She was dressed in flowing blue and white robes, with her long, light-brown hair falling softly over her shoulders. In a few moments the vision ended.

One of the boys ran to tell the Calvinist catechist who ridiculed him and sent him back to the fields to tend the flocks. The other children ran home and told their parents and neighbors about the weeping, heartbroken woman. The sincerity of the children prompted the people to gather at the rock the next morning. Some scoffed, but others fully anticipated a return of the vision.

THE SECOND APPARITION

The Calvinist pastor, aware of the crowd gathering at the place, became alarmed at the gullibility of his people who believed this "Roman superstition." After warning them of this "work of Satan" he was about to leave when he heard the heartrending sound of weeping. Frightened at first, he regained his composure and asked the apparition, "Why are you weeping?" The Blessed Mother replied, "There was a time when my beloved Son was worshipped by my people on this very spot. But now they have given this sacred soil over to the plowman and the tiller and to the grazing animals." Without another word she vanished.

The people quickly regained the Faith so that a decade later, on the Feast of the Nativity of the Blessed Virgin Mary, more than 11,000 people received Holy Communion during a Mass offered at the scene of the apparitions.

The report of the visions gradually reached a very elderly blind man who remembered that the church treasures had been stored in the ground beside a large rock in a field. He was brought to the place he described and was immediately cured of his blindness when he indicated the exact place of the treasure. This miracle had a profound effect on the people.

The chest was dug out of the ground and opened. Everything inside was found perfectly preserved. Having obtained the deeds to the property, the bishop, M. Valancius, petitioned the court for the return of the church and its property. In the year 1622, the Tribunal of Vilnius decided in favor of the Catholics.

Through the years, the church was repeatedly replaced by larger ones to accommodate the people who thronged to venerate the painting of Mother and Child. Now crowned and clad in gold, it is enshrined permanently in the Basilica of the Birth of the Blessed Virgin Mary.

The rock on which the Blessed Mother stood is found in the

"Chapel of the Appearance." It is by the altar where it is accessible to the people, who are permitted to kiss and touch it.

Due to the many favors and miraculous healings received from Our Lady of Siluva, the happenings were extensively investigated by the bishops of the country. The results of their study prompted Pope Pius VI to authenticate the apparitions by a papal decree dated August 17, 1775. It was again authenticated when Pope John Paul II visited Siluva in 1993, and prayed in the Chapel of the Appearance. Finally, Pope Benedict XVI named the Archbishop of Cologne, Germany, to be his special envoy at the 400th anniversary of the apparitions and announced the appointment of Cardinal Joachim Meisner as celebrant for the occasion.

With all these endorsements, Siluva is now regarded as Lithuania's most important Marian shrine.

OUR LADY OF GOOD SUCCESS

Madrid, Spain, Unknown date
Quito, Ecuador, 1610

DISCOVERY OF THE STATUE OF OUR LADY OF GOOD SUCCESS IN MADRID

*T*HROUGHOUT the world, there are many statues that have been given the title of Our Lady of Good Success, but the earliest images known by this title are found in Madrid and Quito. The exact date of the discovery of the Madrid image now under consideration is unknown, although we do know that it begins when Spanish friars were traveling through the village of Traigueras on their way to Rome to gain approval of the Order of Minims founded by St. Francis of Paola (1416–1507). When a furious storm descended upon them, they prayed for God's guidance and help. Looking for shelter, they saw a mysterious light coming from a cave. They hurried to it and found the beautiful statue of the Virgin Mary holding the Child Jesus. Surrounding it was a shimmering light and a heavenly fragrance. When no one in Traigueras knew anything about the statue and did not claim it, the friars carried it with them to Rome. On arriving there, they met with Pope Paul V (1605–1621) who heard the story of the discovery, and not only venerated and blessed the statue, but also gratified the friars by granting full approval of the new Order.

The image was first placed in the Royal Hospital of Madrid

where many miracles were granted, so many, in fact, that King Philip III ordered the construction of the Sanctuary of the Puerto del Sol where the image is found today, beautifully adorned and sumptuously enthroned.

The image of Our Lady of Good Success in Madrid was dear to the hearts of countless souls, including Sr. Mariana of Jesus Torres who, even as a child, received visits of the Blessed Mother. Her great devotion to Our Lady under this title was continued when she arrived in Quito.

THE FIRST VISITATION AT QUITO

After joining the Order of the Immaculate Conception, Sr. Mariana was sent from Spain to Quito to found another house of the Order, of which she became Abbess. It was there on February 2, 1610, while she was praying to the Blessed Mother, that she was granted another heavenly visitation. Identifying herself as Mary of Good Success, the Virgin Mary asked that a statue be made to her likeness for the consolation and preservation of the convent, and for those faithful souls who would pray to her. "With this statue I will favor not only my convent, but also the people of Quito and all the people throughout the centuries."

OTHER APPARITIONS OF THE BLESSED MOTHER

During other apparitions, the Blessed Mother confided several prophecies, some of which have already taken place while many are pertinent to our troubled times. Some of these prophecies include a warning that Masons and other secret sects would have an influence even within the Church. She warned that a worldwide campaign against the virtues of chastity and purity will succeed in corrupting the youth . . .

evil will invade childhood innocence. The clergy
will leave much to be desired because priests will
become careless in their sacred duties . . . Faithful
priests upholding the Faith will suffer greatly and
will be overwhelmed with vexations in order to stop
them from fulfilling their ministry. The precious
light of Faith will be extinguished in souls by the
almost total corruption of customs.

The Lady complained that those who have the financial
means to help the Church do nothing. "Their miserly attitude
toward God and His Church will allow evil to seemingly tri-
umph." Many other prophecies were given which depict the
future as being very troublesome to the Church.

Mother Mariana of Jesus Torres died on January 16, 1635,
after receiving the Holy Eucharist and the Sacraments of the
Church. After three hundred years, in 1906, when the church
was being remodeled, her tomb was opened, revealing her body
perfectly intact. It is now kept in a small chapel in the lower
level of the cloistered convent. Her Cause for beatification was
opened on the diocesan level by the local bishop. At the conclusion of the investigation of her heroic virtues she was given the
title, Servant of God.

At the request of the Blessed Mother, her statue was placed
above the Abbess' chair in the upper choir of the convent because
she desired to be Abbess of the convent "until the end of time."
Unlike the statue in Madrid which depicts the Baby Jesus on her
left arm while the right hand holds a queenly scepter, the statue
in Quito also has the Baby Jesus on the left arm, while the right
hand of the Virgin holds not a royal scepter, but a crosier and the
keys of the convent. The crosier denotes her authority as Abbess.*

---

* Mother Mariana of Jesus Torres should not be confused with
Mariana of Jesus de Paredes Flores also of Quito who is the patron
saint of Ecuador. She was a hermit and is the first saint to be canonized from Ecuador. She was canonized by Pope Pius XII in 1950.

OUR LADY OF MANAOAG

Manaoag, Pangasinan, Philippines
1610

THE FIRST APPARITION AT MANAOAG

OUR Lady's concern for the welfare of the district of Pangasinan was shown in a number of ways: safety from fire, safety of crops from locusts, safety from drought, and also safety from aerial bombardment during World War II. Her love for this region is all-inclusive and inspired wonder in the people, as reported in the district's history.

It all began in 1610, when a man was walking home along a lonely road and happened to hear a Lady's mysterious voice. Turning around, he was greatly surprised to see a radiant Lady holding a small child on one arm while a rosary was suspended from her right hand. The vision was supported by a bright cloud over a small bush. It appears that nothing was said, only the Virgin looking sweetly at the man who was now on his knees in profound reverence.

When the villagers heard of the vision, they hastily journeyed there and soon built a small church over the place of the apparition. A town soon flourished near it which was named Manaoag which means "to call."

MIRACLES OF THE BLESSED VIRGIN

The Blessed Virgin has since protected the area from all manner of injury as she did during the time when the mountain tribes were accustomed to burning Christian villages. One day when Manaoag was destined to be torched, flaming arrows were shot into the little church. Not a single flame set it on fire. On an even greater scale, during World War II, four bombs were dropped. Three landed on the patio and damaged the facade of the church while one bomb fell through the roof but failed to ignite. The church was miraculously saved.

Another wonder was the protection of crops in 1698 from locusts when they began to ravage the rice fields. They came in swarms so big that the sky was darkened. The image of the Blessed Virgin that had been brought to the Philippines in the early seventeenth century by Padre Juan de San Jacinto of Spain, was taken to the fields. Desperate for help, they placed the small image on the ground and watched in amazement as the locusts began to destroy each other in a way totally unexpected and in a way never seen before. The carnage continued until not a single locust could be found.

Still another miracle took place during the drought of 1706, when the fields were scorched by drought and the seedlings were shriveled from the heat. When the sky remained cloudless for days, the people looked to Our Lady for help and took her image once more to the field. During the first day of a novena, and after a procession with the miraculous statue, the Lady showed her compassion by gathering rain clouds as soon as her image was returned to the church. The sky dimmed and a downpour soon fell that continued for days until the ground was refreshed and the crops saved.

Another spectacular miracle of the Lady's was noted in 1698, on Easter Sunday, when a fire of unknown origin devoured the whole town and crept steadily to the church. After the priest of the parish was notified of the danger, he rushed to the scene, went inside and snatched the statue of Our Lady to keep it from harm. He prayed and pleaded with the Lady, saying: "Dear Lady, if you do not spare the church from fire, I will hurl myself into the flames with you so that the two of us may be consumed by it." History notes that the flames immediately died down and were extinguished.

The devotees of Our Lady of Manaoag visit the shrine throughout the year, but especially in April and May when people from all over the world join in annual pilgrimages. The Lady's reputation for favors received is well known and miracles attributed to her are depicted in giant wall paintings in the church. The number of visitors was especially large on April 21, 1926, when the Papal Nuncio canonically crowned the image of Our Lady.

But the people do not always go to her; she also goes to the people when, every twenty-five years, she visits all the barrios of Manaoag and all the towns in the district of Pangasinan. Our Lady has certainly proved her love for the people, and they for her.

COMFORTER OF THE AFFLICTED

Kevelaer, Germany
1641

FIRST APPARITION AT KEVELAER

AT THE time of the apparition, the small village of Kevelaer was a tragic place. A fire had almost completely destroyed it in the late sixteenth century. It was further damaged by the ravages of the Thirty Years' War of 1618–1648 that raged nearby. It was considered a vast moorland and a place where few ventured, but around Christmastime in the year 1641, the Heavenly Mother looked favorably on it.

It all began when Hendrick Busman, a traveling salesman (a tinker), found it necessary to pass that way on his route from the village of Weeze to the neighboring town of Geldern. According to the report to the Synod of Venio, the salesman tells his story:

> My name is Hendrick Busman . . . At Christmas in 1641 I was making my way in the course of my business from the town of Weeze when I came to the region around Kevelaer. There was a cross by the roadside and I heard a voice saying to me, "Here thou shalt build me a chapel."
>
> I heard the voice and looked about me but saw no one. I resolved to press on and put all thoughts of the phenomenon out of my head. About a week later, I passed the place again and there heard the

same voice speaking the same words as before. I heard it again a third time. I was sad because I was poor and I had no means by which I might build a shrine. Nevertheless, I saved regularly from my petty cash in the distant hope that one day I should have a fund to fit the purpose.

Then, four weeks before Whitsunday, my wife, Mechel Schouse, received a vision by night. She saw a great light and in the midst of it a shrine; and in that shrine was a picture of Our Lady of Luxembourg like one she had been shown some time earlier by two soldiers passing through our village. The soldiers had offered to sell Mechel the picture but upon asking the price, she realised she could not afford it.

When Mechel told me of her vision, I connected it with my own experiences near Kevelaer and I urged her to find the soldiers and the picture. She discovered that the picture was now in the possession of a lieutenant presently in prison in Kemen. Mechel obtained the picture from him.

Convinced that the vision experienced by his wife was a confirmation of his Heavenly assignment, Hendrick used the little money he had saved and began to construct a shrine according to Mechel's description, and with the permission of the parish priest of Kevelaer, Rev. Johannes Schink. During its construction, the Carmelite nuns of Geldern heard about the heavenly voice and the vision and asked Hendrick if they might keep the portrait for a time. The portrait was a copper-printed portrait measuring twelve centimeters tall and eight centimeters wide, which depicts Our Lady of Luxembourg, the same Lady who had been worshiped during the pestilence of 1623, as the Comforter of the Sad and Distressed.

When the Carmelite nuns returned the portrait, Hendrick placed it temporarily in his home. This proved a great inconvenience to the household because pilgrims from all over the country wanted to venerate it. Hendrick appealed to the Capuchin priests to place it temporarily in their chapel until the shrine was completed. The crowds of people who went to venerate the image were so great that the monks asked that the holy image be taken as soon as possible to the shrine that was being prepared for it. Finally, when the shrine was completed on June 1, 1642, the priest of Kevelaer, Rev. Johannes Schink, brought the image in great ceremony to the shrine where crowds awaited it.

Miracles were soon reported. On September 8, 1642, Reinier and Margaretha van Volbroek brought their invalid son, Peter, to the shrine. Although his case had been declared hopeless by physicians, Peter was found cured two days after his visit.

Another case involved a woman who had suffered for years with severe lesions on her legs that treatments could not cure. Her healing was so profound that it was reported by the Mayor of Huissen, Holland, who had it recorded by the secretary of the city on August 13, 1643. A new pilgrimage church was started that year. It still exists today and is called the Chapel of Candles.

Before his death in 1649, Hendrick was thankful to see so many pilgrimages making their way to the shrine in accordance with the wishes of Our Lady. Five years later, in 1654, the old chapel he had built was replaced by a new chapel called the Chapel of Mercy. Within this six-sided structure is a pillar from the original chapel which bears an inscription at the base, giving credit to Hendrick and Mechel as founders of the devotion to Our Lady.

The many miracles of healing that took place prompted the Vicar General to order an investigation. As a result, many cures were declared to be miraculous and brought an even greater number of pilgrims to the shrine. In a short time, three Oratorian priests were assigned to help in ministering to the crowds that continually gathered in prayer.

The Basilica was built between the years 1858 and 1864. This, together with the priests' house, the Candle Chapel where hundreds of candles burn each day, the Organizational Center, the Confessional Chapel, the Fountain Courtyard with its bubbling water and the outdoor Stations of the Cross all comprise a huge and beautiful complex that is admired by all who visit.

The little picture of Our Lady, Comforter of the Afflicted, is the source of all attention, especially when it is decorated with golden angels, golden roses, golden medals, chains and jeweled ornaments that have been donated by grateful pilgrims. In 1892, Our Lady was honored with a papal coronation for the 250th anniversary of the shrine's inauguration. During this observance, a crown studded with diamonds and jewels was placed above the miraculous picture.

Among the distinguished persons who visited the image are King Frederick William I, King Frederick William IV and Pope John Paul II. During the pope's visit on May 2, 1987, he stated:

> In great joy I am now come to your shrine in Kevelaer. My first in this pilgrimage to the miraculous image of the Comforter of the Afflicted. Before this picture I have prayed and commended all of you to the special protection of Our Lady. I come as pilgrim and worshiper in the series of countless people since the 1642 pilgrimage to the Blessed Mother in Kevelaer.

Our Lady of the Willow Tree
(Notre-Dame-de-l'Osier)

Vinay, France
1649

*T*HE events relating to the origin of the shrines at Plantées seem beyond belief were it not for the testimony of witnesses, the formal inquiry conducted by the bishop, and the documentation that may still be seen in the Provincial Archives of Grenoble. Finally, the events were given Church approval when, on two occasions, Pope Pius IX ordered the solemn crowning of the statue that had been given the title of Our Lady of the Willow Tree (*Notre-Dame-de-l'Osier*).

The drama of this event involves a farmer of the area, Pierre Port-Combet, who had abandoned the Catholic Faith for the heresy known as Calvinism. While still a Catholic, he had married a devout woman named Jeanne, but after he abandoned the Faith he refused to allow her to raise their six children in the Catholic Faith and instead drew them into heresy.

The village of Plantées at the time was Catholic. According to Church directives all work was to be suspended on Sundays and Church feasts so that all could spend the day in prayer and reflection. It was Pierre's delight to disobey this ruling of the Faith and he continued to work, especially on feast days dedicated to the Blessed Mother.

THE MIRACULOUS EVENT

The miraculous event took place on the Feast of the Annunciation March 25, 1649, when Pierre decided to demonstrate his disdain for the feast by performing work where all would see him. He chose to stand beside a road where the villagers passed on their way to Holy Mass. Pierre drew his knife and pretended to be working by pruning a willow tree that grew beside the road. He stabbed the trunk and drew back in horror. The tree bled, and so much so that it splashed on Pierre's arms and hands. Thinking he was injured, he examined himself but no wound could be found. After a moment of bewilderment he stabbed the tree once more and again the tree bled.

At this moment, his wife was passing by on her way to church and saw blood covering her husband's arms. She hurried to help him, but she too could find no injury. Pierre excitedly related what had happened, and to calm him, she took the knife and struck the tree. Nothing happened. More dismayed than before, Pierre took the knife, struck the tree once again and, as before, the tree bled.

A neighbor passing by, Louis Caillet, was told what happened and tried to produce the same effect, but without success, no matter how many times he tried. All the neighbors who had gathered around the tree agreed that the miracle only took place at the hand of the heretic and that the prodigy was a stern warning for Pierre to convert and observe the laws of the Church.

After the miraculous event at the willow tree, the villagers frequently visited it with great devotion and cut away some of the bark as precious relics.

When Church authorities heard of the case and the prodigy of the blood from the willow, a tribunal of churchmen gathered for a formal inquiry as ordered by the bishop. The testimony of Pierre was taken, as well as that of witnesses. The decision rendered was that Pierre had received a severe warning from Heaven.

Pierre took the decision to heart and was seen occasionally at the willow tree in profound prayer. The Calvinists disapproved of this and even threatened him with bodily harm. For this reason, Pierre's conversion was stalled for seven years, until Our Lady intervened.

OUR LADY INTERVENES TO HASTEN PIERRE'S CONVERSION

On the Feast of the Annunciation, March of the year 1656, in order to appease the Calvinists, he was working in his field when he looked in the distance toward an area known as the Thornhill and saw a Lady clothed in white, wearing a blue mantle. Over her head was a black veil that partially hid her face. As the Lady advanced toward him, Pierre thought she was lost and was coming to him for directions. Displaying amazing speed, the Lady was suddenly standing next to him.

The Lady, in a sweet voice, greeted Pierre: "*A Dieu-sois-tu, mon ami!*" ["God be with you, my friend!"].

Pierre hesitated on hearing the sweet sound of the voice and the beauty of the woman. Again the Lady spoke: "What is being said about this devotion? Do many people come?"

Pierre nervously answered, "Yes, many people come."

Appearing satisfied with Pierre's reply, the Lady continued, "Where does that heretic live who cut the willow tree? Does he not want to be converted?"

Embarrassed by her question, Pierre could only mumble a response. After a moment, the Lady asked: "Do you think I do not know that you are the heretic?" The Lady then gave Pierre this warning:

> Realize that your end is at hand. If you do not
> return to the True Faith you will be cast into Hell.

But if you change your beliefs, I shall protect you
before God. Tell people to pray to advantage, not
to neglect the source of graces which God in His
mercy has made available to them.

After this, the Lady began moving away, but Pierre, overwhelmed with remorse, ran after her to voice his apology and his
willingness to convert. He then saw the Lady suspended several
feet in the air and slowly fading from sight. Realizing that he
had been granted a vision of the Blessed Virgin, he fell to his
knees, and while sobbing uncontrollably, he pledged a complete
reform.

PIERRE'S CONVERSION

One month later, on the eve of the Assumption, Pierre contracted a serious illness. A priest of Vinay heard his Confession
and welcomed him back into the Church. Pierre completed his
conversion by receiving the Holy Eucharist the next day on the
Feast of the Assumption. Pierre's conversion influenced many to
return to the True Faith, including his son and five daughters,
as well as many Protestants and Calvinists. Our Lady's words:
"Realize that your end is at hand . . ." were confirmed weeks
later when Pierre died. In accordance with his final wish, he was
buried at the bottom of the willow tree.

The Propagation of the Faith in Grenoble gave its approval
for the purchase of the field of the apparition and a chapel dedicated to Our Lady of Good Meeting was soon built. This was
replaced by a larger church which was dedicated to Our Lady of
the Willow Tree.

During the French Revolution, terrorists from Grenoble
unfortunately pillaged and desecrated the sanctuary and hacked
to pieces a statue of the Lady that was sculptured according to
Pierre's description. Thankfully, a valiant woman hid the pieces

until peace was restored. A portion of the willow tree was also saved and was stored in a decorative box in the oratory.

Devotion to Our Lady of the Willow Tree was revived following the revolution by the Oblates of Mary Immaculate and in 1856, the second centenary of the apparition, Pope Pius IX decreed a solemn jubilee and a papal crowning of the restored statue on September 8, the birthday of the Immaculate Mary. Another crowning was ordered by the same pontiff in 1873.

The meeting between Our Lady and Pierre is depicted on a large painting in the chapel of Our Lady of Good Meeting. In addition, between the church and the Thornhill, where Our Lady left him, a specially marked path approximately four hundred yards long indicates the route taken by Pierre when he ran after the apparition.

The church built where the willow once grew was raised to the dignity of a minor basilica by Pope Pius XI on March 17, 1924. The once-mutilated statue of Our Lady is found here, and beneath her altar is the decorative box containing the piece of the willow tree, which is located near the same place where it formerly grew. Pierre's tomb is at the foot of this altar.

Many favors and cures have been attributed to prayers before the altar of Our Lady. In fact, more than one hundred cures are said to be undoubtedly genuine since they had been witnessed and sworn to by reliable people who testified under oath and affixed their names to written documents.

Our Lady is especially honored at Plantées on feast days of Our Lady of the Willow, especially on March 25, in observance of the anniversary of the apparition, and on September 8, the birthday of the Blessed Virgin.

OUR LADY OF ETERNAL AID
(OUR LADY OF ALL HELP)

Querrien, La Prenessaye, France
1652

FIRST APPARITION AT QUERRIEN, LA PRENESSAYE, FRANCE

QUERRIEN is a small village located in the northwestern part of France known as Brittany. Here the Blessed Virgin appeared on August 15, to a poor shepherdess, Jeanne Courtel, who was twelve years old. Both deaf and mute since birth, Jeanne was tending her father's flock of sheep and was reciting her prayers when the Blessed Virgin appeared holding the Child Jesus on one arm and holding a stalk of lilies in the other.

The Lady spoke only a few words when Jeanne realized she was miraculously healed and could hear. The Blessed Madonna spoke in a sweet voice, "I choose this place to be honored. Build for me a chapel in the middle of this village and many people will come." Then a dialogue began between the Holy Virgin and the shepherdess. The apparition said, "Charming shepherdess, give me one of your lambs."

Jeanne would willingly have given one to the Lady, but she replied, "These sheep are not mine, they are my father's."

> The Lady then directed, "Return to your parents and tell them that I require a lamb." The girl turned

to leave, but then asked, "But who will keep my herd?" "Myself. I will keep your sheep!"

The little girl returned quickly to her parents who were astonished to hear her speak. Jeanne excitedly told them, "A Lady came to see me, and she asked me for one of your lambs." The father was overjoyed at his child's miraculous recovery, and replied, "Ah, my daughter. Because this Lady has made you speak, we will give her all the flock."

Jeanne also related that the Lady said he should dig the nearby pond to find her statue that had been buried there for centuries. "And did the Lady say who she was?" In utter simplicity Jeanne answered,

> "She said she is the Virgin Mary and we need to build a chapel in the village so many pilgrims will go there to honor her." "If this is true," the father said, "we will ask the bishop to allow us to build a shrine to the Virgin Mary."

In the days that followed, the Virgin appeared again, and repeated her request for a chapel.

History relates that in the year 610, St. Gall had visited the region to erect a hermitage and had sculpted a statue of the Virgin Mary. During a disastrous time in the region, the chapel he built was destroyed, and the statue was lost. But on August 20, having been directed by the Lady to search the pond for the statue, it was duly found and proved to be in excellent condition despite its having been buried in water for centuries.

During the same year of 1652, on September 11, Monsignor Denis de La Barde, bishop of the region, made an appearance and was informed about all that took place. Several days later, on September 20, after conducting his investigation, he formally recognized the validity of the apparitions and blessed the first stone of the future chapel. Begun in 1652, the chapel was completed four years later. Because of the large crowds that visited the shrine, it was enlarged in 1779, and now entombs the body of the visionary, Jeanne Courtel, who died in 1703.

CORONATION OF THE MIRACULOUS STATUE

It is recorded that twenty thousand pilgrims visited Querrien on August 14, 1950, for the coronation of the miraculous statue by the local bishop who did so in the presence of many ecclesiastics.

The year 1968 witnessed the building of a large portico to accommodate outdoor ceremonies and in 1981 a building to house pilgrims was opened.

One of the most splendid ceremonies to take place at the shrine was that in honor of Cardinal Lustiger, Archbishop of Paris, who paid homage to the Madonna and then blessed the new buildings on September 10, 2000. Two years later, the area observed the 350th anniversary of the apparitions of the Virgin of Eternal Aid.

The shrine of Our Lady is proud to announce that it is the only one in Brittany that has been authenticated by the Catholic Church.

OUR LADY OF LAUS

Laus, France
1664

THE visionary of Our Lady of Laus, Benoite Rencurel, was only seven years old when her father died, leaving her family destitute. Born on September 29, 1647, in the region of France known as Saint-Etienne-du-Laus, she helped her mother as much as she could and eventually began tending sheep to help with the family's expenses. Benoite, whose name means "blessed," customarily knelt in the field to recite the Rosary, and was engaged in this devotion during May of 1664, when a venerable man, clothed in the vestments of a bishop of the early Church, appeared to her. He identified himself as St. Maurice, to whom a nearby chapel was dedicated. He directed her to a valley where, he said, she would be visited by the Mother of God.

VISIONS OF THE MOTHER OF GOD

When Benoite and her flock arrived at the place the next morning, she saw a Lady of incomparable beauty holding the hand of a beautiful young Child who stood beside her. Realizing that she, a humble shepherdess, could not possibly be in the company of the Queen of Heaven, she spoke kindly and in a familiarly polite manner. The Lady smiled, but did not reply.

The following day Benoite was again visited by the Mother of God, and for four months the vision appeared every day, talking to Benoite and asking that she pray continually for the conversion of sinners. During this time the Virgin Mary taught the unschooled girl the Litany of Loreto and requested that she teach it to others and to sing it with them each evening in the church.

Soon the apparitions became known and attracted many pilgrims to the site. Because the apparitions continued, the magistrate of Avancon Valley, a Catholic and a man of integrity, conducted a serious examination and concluded that Benoite was not being deceptive. Because of his prompting Benoite asked the Lady to identify herself and was told, "I am Mary, the Mother of Jesus. My Son wishes to be especially honored in this valley."

After four months, the Virgin told Benoite that the apparitions would continue only in the Laus chapel which is located in southern France at the foot of the Alps. Located near her home, the simple chapel was a thatch-roofed structure that looked like all the small houses in the region, which would normally make it difficult to find. But Benoite lost no time in finding it by the sweet fragrance that usually accompanied the visions. On entering, Benoite discovered the beautiful Lady elevated above a dust-covered altar whose only ornaments were two wooden candlesticks and a pewter ciborium.

THE VIRGIN REQUESTS A LARGER CHURCH

The pious mountain people had built the small chapel almost twenty-five years earlier in 1640, and dedicated it to Nôtre-Dame de Bon Rencontre (Our Lady of Good Encounter, meaning Our Lady of the Annunciation). While the Lady was pleased to visit this chapel, she requested that a large church be built with an added building for resident priests, saying that it would ". . . be built in honor of my dear Son and Myself. Here many sinners will be converted. I will appear to you often here . . . and that nothing would be lacking." She reassured Benoite that the new church would be built with the pennies of the poor.

In the year 1665, the Blessed Mother requested that Benoite stop tending flocks in order to devote herself to her mission, which would be to "Pray continually for sinners" and to serve priests who would devote themselves to the sacrament of penance.

Thousands flocked to the once-deserted chapel where graces and blessings poured down upon souls and where many were converted and healed. Soon whole parishes converged there in procession.

CURE OF CATHERINE VIAL

While Masses were permitted to be celebrated in the chapel, the diocesan authorities, including Reverend Canon Pierre Gaillard, the Vicar General of the Diocese, began an inquiry. He was soon convinced of the authenticity of the apparitions, but since Laus belonged to the Diocese of Embrun, Fr. Gaillard was not authorized to pronounce an official judgment. The matter was soon considered by the authorities of Embrun, including several prelates who seriously doubted the validity of all that was happening. However, after witnessing the cure of a well-known cripple, Catherine Vial, all doubts were forgotten. Fr. Gaillard who was a witness wrote, "I am a faithful witness of all that occurred." Another authority declared, "There is something extraordinary occurring in that chapel. Yes, the hand of God is there."

Soon priests were being assigned to minister to the numerous pilgrims and in 1665, authorization was given for the construction of the church that the Blessed Virgin had requested. Because there were no resources for the construction, the poor took up the challenge and despite many irregularities in the landscape that made their walking difficult, the people began carrying stones to the construction site. On October 7, 1666, Feast of the Holy Rosary, the first stone of the building was placed. Witnessing this event was a long procession of pilgrims. Taking advantage of this celebration, Benoite became a Dominican tertiary and from then on she wore the tertiary veil and cape and was called "Sister Benoite."

During the construction, Benoite busied herself in preparing meals for the workers, praying for their safety and making sure all was proceeding as the Blessed Virgin had indicated. Because of her attendance, it is said that not a word of blasphemy was uttered by the workers. To the satisfaction of all, the little thatched-roofed chapel of Nôtre-Dame de Bon Rencontre was incorporated into the structure and became the choir of the new church, which was completed four years later in 1670.

A phenomenon that took place early in the apparitions and continues even to this day is the heavenly perfume that enveloped the area. Historians of Laus are unanimous in reporting the heavenly fragrance that was experienced by many and even spread from the chapel to the valley below. Judge François Grimaud attested,

> During the Easter Season of 1666, I smelled a very sweet fragrance for around seven minutes; I had never smelled anything like it in my life, and it gave me such deep satisfaction that I was enraptured.

A sculptor from Gap, who experienced the fragrance, donated a beautiful statue in Carrara marble, which represents the Virgin and Child. And since the fragrance is often experienced in our day, flowers are not usually allowed at the shrine to prevent any confusion.

The apparitions of Our Lady continued for fifty-four years. Always accompanied by angels, the Lady announced that many miracles would be effected by the application of oil that burned in the lamps of the shrine. Many favors, especially those of healings, were experienced by countless people who heeded the Lady's recommendation.

BENOITE RECEIVES THE STIGMATA

Eventually, Benoite was visited by the suffering Saviour and received the stigmata on a Friday in July 1673. She suffered these wounds from Thursday at four o'clock until Saturday at nine. During her agony, she lay on her bed, her arms extended in the form of a cross, her feet crossed one on the other. According to old documents, she was "as rigid as an iron bar." When this became too much of an attraction to pilgrims, she pleaded with Our Lord that the wounds become invisible. It is uncertain if her prayer in this regard was answered.

On Christmas Day in 1718, it was revealed to her that she would die in three days. In preparation, she made her last Confession, received the last blessings of the Church, said goodbye to those around her and after kissing a crucifix, she died peacefully on December 28. She was seventy-one years old.

The church which Our Lady requested is named, Sanctuaire de Nôtre-Dame-du-Laus and is visited each year by more than 120,000 pilgrims.

FINAL APPROVAL OF THE APPARITION

Final approval of the apparition was given during a Holy Mass celebrated on May 5, 2008. In the presence of the Roman Curia, officials of the Vatican, thirty cardinals and bishops from many countries, Bishop Jean-Michel de Falco of Gap announced:

"I recognize the supernatural origin of the apparitions and the events and words experienced and narrated by Benoite Rencurel. I encourage all of the faithful to come and pray and seek spiritual renewal at this shrine." The bishop continued: "Three hundred forty-four years ago Our Lady chose to address a simple shepherdess to open the way of penitence and conversion, to invite pilgrims to reconcile themselves with the world and with God."

The introduction of the Cause for Benoite's canonization was made on September 7, 1871. In the year 2009, on April 3, the decree of heroic virtues was promulgated by the Vatican. Benoite Rencurel can now be addressed as Venerable.

OUR LADY OF LAS LAJAS

Guaitara Canyon, Colombia
1754

HE portrait of Our Lady of Las Lajas is somewhat like the miraculous tilma of Our Lady of Guadalupe in Mexico City in that the formation of the portraits of Our Lady cannot be explained. Yet both have not lost their brilliance throughout the centuries. Although the tilma of Juan Diego has various kinds of paint, but no brush strokes, that of Las Lajas is different in that no paint or dye was used in its creation. Like the tilma, no brush strokes are visible despite meticulous inspections.

Since the portrait at Las Lajas is attached to a slab of rock, geologists were permitted to bore small holes into the rock in order to find a scientific explanation for its formation. Their conclusion rendered the portrait even more mysterious since they found that the image evenly penetrates into the rock to which it is attached. It would seem that only a heavenly painter performed this beautiful work of art. Historians and scientists cannot explain this mysterious image that may forever remain a mystery.

The history of the portrait involves an Indian woman named Maria Mueses de Quinones who was walking from her village of Potosi to the village of Ipiales. One day in 1754, she was making the journey with her small daughter, Rosa, when she approached the area called Las Lajas (the Rock) where the trail passes through a deep gorge of the Guaitara River. Maria did not like this area since rumor told that the place was haunted. Unexpectedly, a rainstorm started, and spying a cave ahead, she anxiously entered it. While invoking the protection of the Virgin of the Rosary she suddenly felt someone touching her shoulder as though to gain her attention. Without looking back to see who it was, Maria fled back into the storm; Rosa protectively sheltered by her mother's tight embrace.

THE FIRST VISION

Days later, finding it necessary to travel the same route, Maria and Rosa, who was a deaf-mute from birth, paused to rest on a stone near the cave. The first miracle of Our Lady of Las Lajas then took place when the child suddenly spoke. "Mommy, look at the lady with a little boy in her arms." With these words, the child slid off her mother's lap and began to move toward the cave. Struck with terror, Maria grabbed her daughter and rushed from the mysterious place.

On returning home, Maria told friends and neighbors what happened, and all looked in amazement at Rosa who could now speak and hear.

THE SECOND APPARITION

The next day Maria looked for Rosa but could not find her. Remembering what had taken place at the cave, she returned there and found the child kneeling before a beautiful, radiant woman and playing happily with a small child. Realizing at once that she was in the presence of the Blessed Mother and the Child Jesus, Maria knelt in admiration and reverence. The Mother and Child, it seems, had detached themselves temporarily from the miraculous portrait.

Yet another miracle took place when Rosa became very ill and died. Remembering the beautiful Lady and the miracle she had worked in healing the child of her earlier affliction, Maria carried Rosa to the cave and implored the Lady to restore her child to life. Our Lady answered her prayers when the child awoke in perfect health. Friends and neighbors who had seen the child without life were now overwhelmed with awe at this latest miracle and later followed Maria to the apparition site.

Moved at the news of a dead child being restored to life, word spread quickly and far with many visiting the cave, now regarded as a grotto, to ask for answers to their prayers. All were amazed upon entering the grotto to see the delicate and regal image of the Blessed Virgin holding her Infant Son. Pictured with the Mother and Child are St. Dominic on one side who was receiving a rosary from the Virgin, and on the other side is St. Francis of Assisi who is receiving from the Child Jesus the Franciscan cord, which is a symbol of the Franciscan Order. These two Orders, the Dominicans and the Franciscans, are the founders of the two Orders that first evangelized Colombia.

A magnificent church was constructed in such a way as to protect the image, which remains in its original location but can now be found behind the main altar. The location of the church is interesting in that one end was built flat against the hillside of the apparitions while the body of the church spans most of the gorge and is supported by decorative pilings. A bridge from the church touches the adjacent hillside which makes it easier for the approach of pilgrims. Custodians of the church boast that it has more turrets and spires than Notre-Dame in Paris.

Pope Pius XII in 1952 granted a canonical crowning of Our Lady of Las Lajas and in the presence of the entire Colombian episcopate, the Gothic church was elevated to the dignity of a minor basilica.

OUR LADY OF LA VANG

La Vang, Vietnam
1798

INTRODUCTION OF CATHOLICISM TO VIETNAM

IN THE sixteenth century, as in the twentieth, there were disputes about the separation of the northern and southern parts of Vietnam. The early history tells that the Trinh family ruled the northern region while the Le and Nguyen families governed the southern portion. Finally, war broke out between them. When the Nguyen family in the south opened their part of the country to foreign merchant ships in exchange for guns and ammunition, Catholicism was introduced. Father Diego Aduarte, a Dominican, came aboard a Spanish merchant ship in 1593, and established a mission in Ding Cat.

Later, the Jesuits came, and with the increase of Catholics, thirty-seven parishes were established. Catholicism was marginally tolerated because of the country's relations with European powers, such as France, Spain and Portugal. Despite the many conflicts between them, the Nguyen dynasty somehow reunited the north and south into a unified Vietnam.

The persecution of Catholics dates back to 1640, when the Nguyen lords grew displeased with Spanish merchants and killed two missionaries. Other priests were expelled and many Catholics were martyred. Periodic persecutions of the Vietnamese Catholics continued and escalated in 1798, after the Nguyen

Dynasty decreed that Catholicism was introduced by foreigners with the purpose of recruiting and influencing the working class against them. Direct attacks were then aimed at all thirty-seven parishes. Needless to report, many of the faithful died as martyrs.

Because of the magnitude of the persecution many Catholics retreated to the jungle where they suffered hunger and sickness and prepared themselves for martyrdom. Several Catholics near La Vang also retreated to the jungle where they were threatened by bitter cold, wild animals, and starvation. One night, as was their custom, they were saying the Rosary and the Mother of God appeared. To their astonishment, they beheld the beautiful Lady who wore a long cape over her gown and was holding a beautiful Child in her arms. Two angels stood prayerfully on either side.

She was immediately recognized as the Blessed Mother. The Lady recommended that they boil the leaves from the surrounding ferns (La Vang means ferns) to use as medicine. She told them that those who prayed there would be heard by her and their petitions answered. All who were present saw the apparition. When they were able, the people erected a small chapel in her honor. As reports of the apparition spread, many journeyed to the place, despite its isolated location in the high mountains.

BISHOP GASPAR ORDERS THE BUILDING OF A CHURCH

After the persecution the bishop of La Vang, Bishop Gaspar, ordered that a church be built in the place of the apparition in honor of the Lady of La Vang. Because of its location on a high mountain, it took many years to complete. Finally, when the church was dedicated by the bishop, he proclaimed during the solemn ceremony that the Lady of La Vang was the Protector of the Catholic communities.

An even larger church was built in 1928, that was unfortunately destroyed in the summer of 1972, during the Vietnam War.

With the validation of many cures and favors, another more beautiful church was built. This was elevated by Pope John XXIII to a minor basilica while on June 19, 1988, Pope John Paul II, in canonizing 117 Vietnamese martyrs, recognized the importance and significance of Our Lady to the Vietnamese people. The following year, for the 200th anniversary of the apparition, Pope John Paul II, in writing to Cardinal Paul Joseph Pham Dinh Tun, Archbishop of Vietnam, wrote: "I warmly join in the joy and thanksgiving of the Bishops of Vietnam and the members of the dioceses."

The sanctuary is an important site of pilgrimage for Catholics in Vietnam, as well as for the Catholic Overseas Vietnamese Community. To accommodate the pilgrims the La Vang Boarding House was recently constructed. The Vietnamese people have dedicated many churches in the United States to Our Lady of La Vang where she remains their beautiful champion to whom they freely give their love and reverence.

OUR LADY OF LICHEN

Lichen, Poland
1813 and 1950

THE FIRST VISION

DURING a time when Polish soldiers were fighting with the French under Napoleon, a fierce battle took place in Leipzig, Germany, in 1813. One of the Polish soldiers, Tomasz Klossowski was seriously wounded. If he were to die, he wanted to do so in his native land. While praying fervently to Our Lady for this intention, the Queen of Heaven appeared to him. Holding a white dove, the vision wore a gown with a golden mantle and a golden crown upon her head. She comforted the soldier and promised he would recover and return to Poland. In addition, she asked him to find a portrait of her that resembled the apparition.

Just as she had promised, the soldier recovered and returned to his home near Lichen. Year after year he tried to find the image requested by the Lady and wandered about the countryside searching for it. Eventually, in 1836, he found it in the village of Lgota. The portrait was first placed in his home, but wanting others to be inspired by the Holy Mother, he hung it on a pine tree in the forest, beside a well-traveled path.

An Episcopal committee examined the details of the apparition and decided to move the portrait to the parish church in Lichen. This took place in 1852. Church records reveal that in

1939, three thousand answers to prayers were recorded, including miraculous recoveries. Unhappily, it is also recorded that during World War II, both the church and the rectory were confiscated and used by the Nazi Youth Organization. Fortunately, the portrait was hidden and preserved.

VISION TO MIKOLAJ SIKATKA

In 1950, the Blessed Virgin revealed herself to the shepherd, Mikolaj Sikatka, who was pasturing cattle near the image. In her message she exhorted people to conversion and to break from greed and sinfulness. She requested that they pray the Rosary and that priests should celebrate the liturgy worthily and reverently. Finally, she requested that her image be moved to a more fitting place. The Lady predicted that a church and monastery in Lichen would be built in her honor and warned that if her message were not accepted a terrible plague would punish the land for its obstinacy.

Mikolaj, the poor shepherd, spread the message as best he could, but was persecuted and even imprisoned because of it by the Russian invaders. The people scoffed at him, but two years later when, according to Mary's prophecy, a cholera epidemic broke out, they remembered the Virgin's warning and flocked to the image to pray the Rosary for the sick and dying.

As Our Lady had predicted, a marvelous shrine was built and was entrusted to the care of the Marian Fathers (the Marians of the Immaculate Conception), who administer the National Shrine of the Divine Mercy in Stockbridge, Massachusetts. This church was consecrated by Cardinal Stefan Wyszynski, the Primate of Poland, who crowned the miraculous image in the presence of several bishops, hundreds of priests, religious and approximately 150,000 laypeople.

Built entirely by the contributions of pilgrims, the

architecturally splendid church that stands today was consecrated by Pope John Paul II on June 7, 1999. It is rightly claimed to be one of the largest and most beautiful in the world. To this day, the recommendation of the Virgin Mary that all should convert and avoid sin is heeded since the majority of pilgrims receive the Sacrament of Reconciliation. So many, in fact, that the pilgrimage center seems to have been built specifically for the reception of the Sacrament.

Our Lady of the Miraculous Medal

Paris, France
1830

CATHERINE LABOURÉ ENTERS RELIGIOUS LIFE

CATHERINE Labouré, the visionary of the Miraculous Medal, was born May 2, 1806, into a large farming family in the peaceful village of Fain-les-Moutiers, France. Her mother died when Catherine was nine years old, and it was then that she chose the Blessed Mother for her mother and protector. Her sister Tonine tells that after Catherine's First Holy Communion "she withdrew more from the playful life of childhood into a solemnity beyond her years. She had no time for games and she became entirely mystic." She was accustomed to attending daily Mass at the chapel that was more than a mile from her home and is known to have declined two marriage proposals. In an effort to discourage his daughter from entering the religious life, her father sent her to live with a brother who conducted a restaurant in Paris, and there she waited on tables. When Catherine was twenty-three years old and no longer needed the permission of her father, she entered the Order of the Daughters of Charity in January of 1830, at Catillon-sur-Seine. Three months later, she was transferred to the Mother House on the Rue du Bac in Paris. As a postulant, she humbly attended to household chores and studied the Rule and Statutes of the Order.

CATHERINE BEHOLDS OUR LORD, ST. VINCENT DE PAUL AND THE BLESSED MOTHER

From the early days of her religious life, she frequently beheld Our Lord in front of the Blessed Sacrament during Mass. On three occasions, she saw mystical symbolic visions of St. Vincent de Paul, the founder of the order, above the reliquary containing his incorrupt heart, which is still enshrined in the chapel of the motherhouse. Undoubtedly, the most extraordinary visions were those of Our Blessed Mother.

The First Vision

On the eve of the Feast of St. Vincent de Paul, July 18, 1830, Catherine was awakened during the night by her angel, who appeared as a child of about five years old, all radiant with light. In a voice deeper in tone than children of that age, the angel announced, "Sister Labouré, come to the chapel, the Blessed Virgin awaits you."

Catherine gently protested, saying, "We shall be discovered."

To this the angel replied, "Do not be uneasy, it is half-past eleven, everyone is sleeping. Come, I am waiting for you."

Catherine dressed quickly and on entering the hallway, she was amazed to see the lights burning brightly. After the angel opened the door to the chapel with a gentle touch, Catherine found the chapel ablaze with lights as if prepared for Midnight Mass.

St. Catherine tells us what happened next.

> The child led me into the sanctuary near the director's chair. And there I knelt down and the child remained standing. As I found the time dragging, I looked around . . . Finally the child alerted me. He

said to me: "Here is the Blessed Virgin—here she is!" I heard a sound like the rustling of a silk dress which came from near the picture of St. Joseph. The Blessed Mother then approached the altar steps at the Gospel side and gracefully sat down on the chair which is kept there. I sprang forward with one leap to her side—kneeling with my hands resting on the knees of the Blessed Virgin. There I spent the sweetest moments in my life. It would be impossible for me to tell all that I experienced.

In a voice of profound respect the angel then whispered in a voice much deeper, "The Blessed Mother wishes to speak with you." The Vision sadly announced,

> God wishes to charge you with a mission. You will be contradicted, but do not fear, you will have the grace to do what is necessary. Tell your spiritual director all that passes within you. Times are evil in France and in the world. Come to the foot of the altar. Graces will be shed on all, great and little, especially upon those who seek for them. You will have the protection of God and Saint Vincent. I will always have my eyes upon you. There will be much persecution. The Cross will be treated with contempt. It will be hurled to the ground and blood will flow. The whole world will be in an upheaval due to all sorts of troubles . . . Come to the foot of this altar. There graces will be shed upon all those who ask for them with confidence and fervor.

Then, after secretly confiding other matters to the little postulant, the vision slowly disappeared. Catherine then followed the angel through the hallway to the dormitory where the angel disappeared. As she slipped into bed, Catherine heard the clock strike two.

This is the only instance in which a visionary touched the sacred body of the Queen of Heaven and the only time in which the visionary spent two hours in intimate conversation with her.

The Second Vision

During the same year, on November 27, at about 5:30 p.m. during the community's time of meditation, Catherine was in the chapel with the other sisters when she recognized the swish of silk. Catherine tells what then transpired:

> Turning in that direction, I saw the Blessed Virgin, at the level of St. Joseph's picture. The Virgin was standing. She was of medium height, and clothed all in white. Her dress was of the whiteness of the dawn, made in the style called "a la Vierge," that is, high neck and plain sleeves. A white veil covered her head and fell on either side to her feet. Under the veil her hair, in coils, was bound with a fillet ornamented with lace, about three centimeters in height or of two fingers' breadth, without pleats and resting lightly on the hair. Her face was sufficiently exposed, indeed exposed very well, and so beautiful that it seems to me impossible to express her ravishing beauty. Her feet rested on a white globe and there was also a serpent, green in color with yellow spots.
>
> Her hands were raised to the height of the stomach and held, in a very relaxed manner and as if offering it to God, a golden ball surmounted with a little golden cross, which represented the world. Her eyes were now raised to Heaven, now lowered. Her face was of such beauty that I could not describe it.

All at once I saw rings on her fingers, three rings to each finger, the largest one near the base of the finger, one of medium size in the middle, the smallest one at the tip. Each ring was set with gems, some more beautiful than others; the larger gems emitted greater rays and the smaller gems, smaller rays; the rays bursting from all sides flooded the base, so that I could no longer see the feet of the Blessed Virgin.

The Blessed Mother then explained that the gems are, "the symbols of the graces I shed upon those who ask for them."

The golden globe that the Virgin held slowly disappeared and there appeared around the Virgin an oval frame on which brilliant gold letters read, "O Mary, conceived without sin pray for us who have recourse to thee." The vision reversed itself and there appeared the Virgin's monogram, a cross intertwined and an "M" which is found on the back of the Miraculous Medal. Under the monogram are the flaming hearts of the Sacred Heart surrounded with thorns, and the Immaculate Heart of Mary pierced with a sword. In the oval frame the whole is surrounded by twelve stars which represent the vision of St. John in the Book of Revelation (12:1).

The vision then said, "Have a medal struck after this model. All who wear it will receive great graces; they should wear it around the neck. Graces will abound for those who wear it with confidence."

The Third Vision

The third vision was almost identical to the second, except that the Virgin moved to a position above and behind the tabernacle, which place is now occupied by a statue made in the likeness of the vision.

The privileged soul reported these visions only to her superior and her spiritual director, and many difficulties had to be overcome before the medals were made and distributed. Because of the many favors received the medal quickly became known as "Miraculous."

After her profession, Catherine was assigned to the hospice on the Rue de Reuilly, where she spent the next forty-six years of her life performing menial tasks for the aged, sick and infirm. While all the sisters were aware that one in their midst was the celebrated visionary of the Miraculous Medal, Catherine's identity was not made known until she was on her deathbed. Having often predicted that she would never see the year 1877, Catherine died on December 31, 1876.

Canonized on July 27, 1947, St. Catherine's body remains incorrupt in a crystal-sided reliquary in the chapel of the motherhouse at 140 Rue du Bac in Paris. Also found in the chapel is the chair on which Our Lady sat during the first vision.*

---

* Although the Blessed Virgin asked only that the medal be worn, no special devotions were requested. However, the Association of the Miraculous Medal in Perryville, Maryland, conducts a monthly novena in her honor.

OUR LADY OF THE MIRACLE
(OUR LADY OF ZION)

Rome, Italy
1842

MARIE Alphonse Ratisbonne was the son and heir of a wealthy, aristocratic Jewish family of bankers. While he was still a child an older brother converted to Catholicism and became a priest. Ratisbonne resolved then to avoid his brother and never speak to him again, and developed a passionate hatred of the Catholic religion.

At the age of twenty-eight, he was engaged to his own niece, and was scheduled to assume a partnership at his uncle's bank. During the engagement, he decided to tour some of Europe for health reasons and pleasure, and was on his way to spend the winter in Malta when his travel plans were unexpectedly changed. Instead of Malta, he arrived in Rome.

While walking through the streets of the ancient city, he encountered a former Protestant classmate, Gustavo de Bussieres. In the process of rekindling their friendship he met Gustavo's brother, Baron Theodore de Bussieres who was a convert to Catholicism and a close friend of Alphonse's priest-brother. Immediately, Alphonse felt a repulsion toward the Baron, a zealous Catholic whose mission was to convert every Jew he met. Since, by a coincidence, they would both be going to Constantinople, Alphonse tolerated his friendship.

The Baron, eager to convert his new friend, challenged Alphonse to a little test. This consisted of wearing a Miraculous

Medal and reciting every day the Memorare, a prayer composed by St. Bernard to the Blessed Mother. Alphonse smilingly agreed, knowing that his hatred for the Faith would shield him from all influences toward a reversal of his Jewish beliefs. Determined to win him over, the Baron sought out his friends, many of whom were converts themselves, to pray for the conversion of the young Jew.

THE FIRST VISION

Soon after, when the Baron was arranging the funeral of a friend in the church of St. Andrea delle Fratte in Rome, he brought Alphonse with him to the church and asked him to wait while he consulted the priest. In a short time, he returned and found Alphonse on his knees reciting the Memorare through abundant tears. Alphonse tells what happened:

> I was scarcely in the Church when a total confusion came over me. When I looked up, it seemed to me that the entire Church had been swallowed up in shadow, except one chapel. It was as though all the light was concentrated in that single place. I looked over towards this chapel whence so much light shone, and above the altar was a living figure, tall, majestic, beautiful and full of mercy. It was the Most Holy Virgin Mary resembling her figure on the Miraculous Medal. At this sight I fell on my knees right where I stood. Unable to look up because of the blinding light, I fixed my glance on her hands, and in them I could read the expression of mercy and pardon. In the presence of the Most Blessed Virgin Mary, even though she did not speak a word to me, I understood her perfectly. I realized the frightful situation I was in, my sins, and the beauty of the Catholic Faith.

Weak from his experience, the Baron helped him to his hotel where Alphonse sobbed uncontrollably and asked, "When can I receive Baptism without which I can no longer live?" He took off the Miraculous Medal and held it up crying, "I saw Her! I saw Her!"

ALPHONSE IS CONVERTED

When he recovered, the Baron took him to a Jesuit retreat house where Alphonse received instruction under the guidance of a Father Villefort. Then, at the hands of His Eminence Cardinal Patrizi, the Vicar of His Holiness, Alphonse was baptized, confirmed and received his First Holy Communion.

The following month, the Vatican began a canonical process to investigate the circumstances of the conversion and, after many interviews and depositions, it determined that the conversion was altogether miraculous.

A few months later, a picture of the Madonna of the Miracle was painted according to Alphonse's description, and was placed for veneration in the same place where she had appeared.

That same year, Cardinal Patrizi declared the conversion to be a divine miracle and permitted the publication of texts recording the event.

THE SISTERHOOD OF OUR LADY OF ZION IS FOUNDED

After his conversion, Alphonse Ratisbonne reconciled with his brother, the priest, and assisted him in founding the Sisterhood of Our Lady of Zion.

The conversion of Ratisbonne was so complete that he studied for the priesthood and was ordained as a member of the

Society of Jesus. He eventually left the Society with the consent of Pope Pius IX to assist the Sisters of Zion for whom he built, in Jerusalem, a large convent, a school and an orphanage for girls. Another convent was established on the mountain at Ain Karim together with a church and another orphanage for girls. Alphonse stayed there for the rest of his life and labored with a few companions for the conversion of Jews and Muslims. He died on May 6, 1884.

Because of the many miracles worked at the shrine where the apparition took place, and where Our Lady's portrait is displayed, Pope Leo XIII visited there in 1892, to crown the Holy Virgin with a splendid diadem. Pope Pius XII elevated the church to the rank of a basilica while Pope John XXIII in 1960, elevated the basilica of the vision, Sant Andrea delle Fratte, to the title of a Cardinal's Church. The third pope to recognize the miraculous conversion and the apparition was Pope John Paul II who visited the basilica on February 28, 1982.

OUR LADY OF LA SALETTE

Corps, Grenoble, France
1846

THE ONLY APPARITION AT LA SALETTE

THIS apparition occurred only once. In it the Blessed Mother predicted consequences regarding the condition of France as it then existed, and terrible revelations for the future of the world, especially those that relate to the Antichrist. Our Lady has always been one of few words, but this vision was an exception. This time she spoke at length and shed many tears.

The visionaries were two children, Melanie Calvat, aged fourteen, and Maximin Giraud, aged eleven years, who lived in the little village of Corps not far from Grenoble in France. They were employed as cowherders and were climbing the slopes of Mont sous-les-Baisses, urging the cows along, when they came upon a bright light, which Melanie described as being brighter than the sun. She tells us, "I felt full of tremendous loving wonder and respect. In that light I saw a very beautiful woman sitting on a rock, her elbows on her knees and her hands covering her face." The lady stood up, crossed her arms in the sleeves of her gown and said, "Come nearer, children, do not be afraid, I am here to tell you great news." The children were amazed to see that the Lady looked very sad and had tears streaming down her cheeks.

The lady's clothing was very different from that which she had worn in previous apparitions and those that followed. The hem of the shawl around her shoulders was lined with roses of various colors and a heavy chain. Around the neck was a smaller chain that supported a crucifix on which was attached on either side a pair of pinchers and a hammer. Her crown was composed of roses that emitted long sparks of light.

She spoke tearfully of wanting the people to repent, that they should stop blaspheming and working on Sundays. The lady then revealed,

> If my people will not obey, I shall be compelled to loose my Son's arm. It is so heavy, so pressing that I can no longer restrain it. How long I have suffered for you! If my Son is not to cast you off, I am obliged to entreat Him without ceasing. But you take no least notice of that. No matter how well you pray in the future, no matter how well you act, you will never be able to make up to me what I have endured for your sake.
>
> You have been appointed six days for working. The seventh I have reserved for myself. And no one will give it to me. This it is which causes the weight of my Son's arm to be so crushing. The cart drivers cannot swear without bringing in my Son's name. These are the two things which make my Son's arm so burdensome.
>
> If the harvest is spoiled, it is your own fault. I warned you last year by means of the potatoes. You paid no heed. Quite the reverse, when you discovered that the potatoes had rotted, they swore, they abused my Son's name. The potatoes will continue to rot and by Christmas this year there will be none left. If you have grain, it will do no good to sow it, for what you sow the beasts will devour, and any part of it that springs up will crumble into dust when you thresh it. A great famine is coming. But before that happens, the children under seven years

of age will be seized with trembling and die in their parents' arms. The grownups will pay for their sins by hunger. The grapes will rot, and the walnuts will turn bad.

OUR LADY GIVES THE CHILDREN A SECRET

The Lady then gave each of the children a secret which Melanie wrote down as instructed by the Lady. (She handed this document to Pope Pius IX in 1851.)

Then, with a searching look, the Vision asked, "Do you say your prayers well, my children?" Melanie and Maximin both agreed, "We say them hardly at all."

> "Ah, my children," the lady replied, "it is very important to say them, at night and in the morning. When you don't have time, at least say an Our Father and a Hail Mary. And when you can, say more."

Another question was asked by the Lady, "My children, haven't you ever seen spoiled grain?" Maximin answered, "No, never." Then, revealing how much Our Lady looks after us, she reminded him:

> "But my child, you must have seen it once, near Coin, with your papa. The owner of a field said to your papa, 'Come and see my spoiled grain.' The two of you went. You took two or three ears of grain in your fingers. You rubbed them, and they crumbled to dust. Then you came back from Coin. When you were but a half hour away from Corps, your papa gave you a piece of bread and said, 'Well, my son, eat some bread this year. I don't know what we will be eating next year if the grain goes on spoiling like that.'"

Maximin answered, "Now I remember it. Until now I did not."

Then speaking of future events the Lady warned,

> Woe to the inhabitants of the earth! God will exhaust His anger. The heads, the leaders of the people of God have neglected prayer and penance, and the devil has darkened their minds; they have become those wandering stars which the ancient devil will drag with his tail to destruction. God will permit the ancient serpent to sow divisions among the rulers, in all societies and in all families; both physical and moral punishments will be suffered. God will abandon men to themselves and will send chastisements one after the other.

The Lady continued that churches would be closed and priests and religious would be driven out. "Many will abandon the faith and the number of priests and religious who will separate themselves from the true religion will be great; even bishops will be found among these persons."

The Lady spoke about a great many devils being loosed from Hell, of bad books leading many to perdition, of false doctrine being preached, of wars, blood in the street and of the Antichrist.

> It will be at this time that the Antichrist will be born of a Hebrew nun, a false virgin who will be in communication with the ancient serpent, master of impurity; his father will be a bishop. At birth he will vomit blasphemies . . . this will be the devil incarnate. The seasons will be changed, the earth will produce only bad fruits, the heavenly bodies will lose the regularity of their movements, the moon will reflect only a feeble reddish light; water and fire will lend convulsive motions to the earth's sphere, causing mountains, cities and more to be swallowed up.

Rome will lose the Faith and become the seat of the Antichrist. The demons of the air, together with the Antichrist, will work great wonders on the earth and in the air, and men will become even more perverted. God will take care of His faithful servants and men of good will; the Gospel will be preached everywhere, all people and all nations will have knowledge of the Truth.

Woe to the inhabitants of the earth. There will be bloody wars, and famines; plagues and contagious diseases; there will be frightful showers of animals; thunders will demolish cities; earthquakes which will engulf countries; voices will be heard in the air; men will beat their heads against the walls; they will call on death, yet death will constitute their torment; blood will flow on all sides. Who could overcome, if God does not shorten the time of trial? At the blood, tears and prayers of the righteous, God will relent; . . . the fires of Heaven will fall and consume three cities; the whole universe will be struck with terror, and many will allow themselves to be seduced because they did not adore the true Christ living in their midst. It is time; the sun is darkening; Faith alone will survive.

The time is at hand; the abyss is opening. Here is the king of darkness. Here is the beast with its subjects, calling itself the savior of the world. In pride he will rise skyward to go up to Heaven; he will be stifled by the breath of St. Michael the Archangel. He will fall and the earth, which for three days will be in constant change, will open its fiery bosom; he will be plunged forever with all his followers into Hell's eternal chasms. Then water and fire will purify the earth and consume all the works of men's pride, and everything will be renewed; God will be served and glorified.

After speaking about the Antichrist and all that would take place in the last days, she concluded, "The time is at hand, the abyss is opening . . . You will tell this to all my people."

While the Blessed Mother spoke these words, she slowly walked up the hill and vanished. There can now be found three statues along the path she took: the first depicts her sitting on the rock weeping, the second while she was speaking to the children, and the third as she is ascending into Heaven following the apparition.

Both children described how the Lady disappeared: that she rose slightly in the air and then slowly vanished before their eyes. Melanie related later, "She must be a great saint. If we had known that we would have asked her to take us with her."

When Maximin was of age, he studied for the priesthood, but realized the lack of a vocation and remained a layman. He died on March 1, 1875, at forty years of age. Melanie lived in various convents and died on December 15, 1904.

THE BISHOP DECLARES BELIEF IN THE VISION

After carefully studying all the aspects of the apparition, the bishop of the diocese, Bishop de Bruillard of Grenoble, announced in 1851, "We declare that the apparition of the Blessed Virgin to two children, on September 19, 1846, on a mountain in the Alps in the parish of La Salette, bears in itself all the marks of truth and that the faithful are justified in believing without question in its truth. And so, to make our lively gratitude to God and the glorious Virgin Mary, we authorize the cult of Our Lady of La Salette.*

---

* The reader is strongly encouraged to read the full text of Our Lady's message, which is too long to present here. It can be found at http://www.catholicapologetics.info/catholicteaching/privaterevelation/lasalet.html or write to the author for a copy or make a search on Google.

The devotion was further confirmed by many popes since the time of Pius IX. In 1942, a Mass and an office were authorized.

A grand basilica was completed in 1879, and was consecrated by the Cardinal Archbishop of Paris, acting as the delegate of the Holy Father. He also crowned the statue representing Mary as she had appeared more than thirty years before to the two young cowherders.

OUR LADY OF LOURDES

Lourdes, France
1858

THE most visited shrine of the Blessed Mother in the world is that of Our Lady of Lourdes in southern France. It is reported that more than a million people visit the shrine each year.

Lourdes was a small, obscure village in the French foothills of the Pyrenees when fourteen-year-old Bernadette Soubirous was gathering firewood at a place known as Massabielle. This was a dark, rocky place with a grotto covered with clumps of bushes. The place was generally looked upon with disfavor but sometimes shepherds sought the area as protection for their sheep. It was in the hollow of the massive rock that the Virgin Mother appeared on February 11, 1858.

THE FIRST VISION

The visionary of Our Lady, Bernadette Soubirous, was born on January 7, 1844, and was always a weak child, suffering almost all her life from asthma. She was also a poor student in school.

The Blessed Virgin would appear to Bernadette eighteen times with the last visitation taking place on July 16 of the same year. Only Bernadette saw the apparition, and only Bernadette heard her. Bernadette herself tells us what took place.

I heard a great noise like the sound of a storm. I looked to the right, to the left, under the trees of the river, but nothing moved; I thought I was mistaken . . . I was frightened and stood straight up. I lost all power of speech and thought when, turning my head toward the grotto, I saw at one of the openings of the rock a rosebush, one only, moving as if it were very windy. Almost at the same time there came out of the interior of the grotto a golden-colored cloud, and soon after a Lady, young and beautiful, exceedingly beautiful, the like of whom I had never seen, came and placed herself at the entrance of the opening above the rosebush. She looked at me immediately, smiled at me and signed to me to advance, as if she had been my mother. All fear had left me but I seemed to know no longer where I was. I rubbed my eyes, I shut them, I opened them; but the Lady was still there continuing to smile at me and making me understand that I was not mistaken. Without thinking of what I was doing, I took my rosary in my hands and went on my knees. The Lady made a sign of approval with her head and herself took into her hands a rosary which hung on her right arm. When I attempted to begin the rosary and tried to lift my hand to my forehead, my arm remained paralyzed, and it was only after the Lady had signed herself that I could do the same. The Lady left me to pray all alone; she passed the beads of her rosary between her fingers but she said nothing; only at the end of each decade did she say the Gloria with me. When the recitation of the rosary was finished, the Lady returned to the interior of the rock and the golden cloud disappeared with her.

It is significant that the Lady remained silent except for the recitation of the "Gloria." It would have been inappropriate for her to ask the Father for her daily bread, and she would surely not salute herself by reciting the Hail Mary. She would, of course, be quite willing to give praise to the Holy Trinity with the recitation of the "Gloria."

As to the appearance of the Lady, Bernadette tells us in detail:

> She has the appearance of a young girl of sixteen or seventeen. She is dressed in a white robe, girdled at the waist with a blue ribbon which flows down all around it. A yoke closes in graceful pleats at the base of the neck; the sleeves are long and tight-fitting. She wears upon her head a veil which is also white; this veil gives just a glimpse of her hair and then falls down at the back below her waist. Her feet are bare but covered by the last folds of her robe except at the point where a yellow rose shines upon each of them. She holds on her right arm a rosary of white beads with a chain of gold shining like the two roses on her feet.

The Blessed Virgin is said to be a person of few words. During some of the apparitions she said nothing, but during one of the early visitations the Virgin told Bernadette, "I cannot promise to make you happy in this world, only in the next." During the fifth vision, the Lady taught Bernadette a prayer that she continued to recite daily, although she never revealed the words. She was also given three secrets which she never revealed. These are thought to have been about her future and what she could expect. She was told during one of the early apparitions that she should bring a blessed candle with her when she returned to the grotto and even though the civil authorities attempted to prevent her from returning, she continued to do so for her daily apparitions.

During the sixth apparition, Bernadette received the injunction, "Pray for sinners."

The seventh apparition lasted almost an hour. Towards the end Bernadette did something unusual by moving, while still on her knees, from the spot where she had been praying to beneath the wild rose bush that grew under the hollow where the lady stood. She kissed the ground and returned, while still on her knees, to the place she had left. Bernadette later confided that the Lady had told her something which she could not reveal.

During the eighth apparition, the Virgin said three times, "Penance! Penance! Penance!"

The ninth visit was extraordinary since Bernadette was told, "Drink from the fountain and bathe in it." Because there had never been a fountain at Massabielle or any kind of natural spring, Bernadette began to scratch the ground until a little pool of water appeared. She cupped her hands together and drank; afterward, she washed her face in the muddy water. She was also asked by the Lady to eat of the grasses, which Bernadette did willingly. The next day the pool was overflowing. It is water from this spring that is distributed throughout the world. This same water has proved to be miraculous in many documented cases.*

During the thirteenth apparition, the Blessed Mother asked Bernadette to contact the clergy. It was the Lady's desire that a chapel should be built and that people should come to this chapel in processions.

Members of the family and countless visitors had implored Bernadette several times to ask the identity of the Lady. Bernadette had done so, but the Lady had not responded. During the sixteenth apparition on March 25, 1858, the Feast of the Annunciation, Bernadette asked once more. This time the Lady responded in the Bigourdane dialect, "*Que soy era Immaculada Conceptiou*," which means, "I am the Immaculate Conception."

In the year 1854, four years *before* the start of the apparitions

---

* To receive some of this water write to Lourdes Center, Marist Fathers, Lourdes Bureau, P.O. Box 15575, Boston, MA 02215-2594. Kindly enclose a donation to cover expenses and postage.

at Lourdes, Pope Pius IX had declared the doctrine of the Immaculate Conception of the Virgin Mary to be an "article of faith" to be believed by all Catholics. The doctrine was neither understood nor discussed among persons of Bernadette's station in life, so it was reasonable that Bernadette did not understand the words spoken by the Lady.

During the seventeenth apparition, while Bernadette was in an ecstatic trance, the people saw the miracle of the lighted candle. Holding the candle in her left hand, as she always did during the apparitions, she moved the right hand over the flame and remained in that position for several minutes. She did not flinch from pain nor was her hand damaged.

The eighteenth and last apparition took place on Friday, July 16, 1858.

The approval of the apparitions was not long in coming since four years after the last visitation, the bishop of the diocese declared the faithful to be "justified in believing the reality of the apparitions." The basilica that was built at the Lady's request was consecrated and the statue that had been placed in the hollow of the rock was solemnly crowned. Another church was built, The Church of the Rosary. Pope Leo XIII authorized an office and a Mass in commemoration of the apparition while Pope Pius X in 1907, authorized the feast to be observed throughout the entire Church on February 11, the anniversary of the first apparition.

After the apparitions, Bernadette became a Sister of Charity of Nevers and was frequently visited by those who wanted her to recite the contents of the apparitions. She lived in the convent for thirteen years, spending much of her time in the infirmary, suffering from tuberculosis of the bone in the right knee, the disease that would claim her life on April 16, 1879. Her incorrupt body can be viewed in a reliquary of gold and glass in the chapel of the motherhouse in Nevers, France.

Every day in Lourdes the wishes of the Lady are realized, with thousands participating in candlelight processions. Many of these are the sick and lame praying for the motherly consideration of the Blessed Virgin. They not only drink of the miraculous water, but also dip themselves into tubs of water, praying for a cure. Many of these prayers have been answered, according to physicians who examined each case previous to and after each cure.*

---

* To pay a visit to the grotto by way of a live transmission please log onto: http://fr.lourdes-france.org.

OUR LADY OF GOOD HELP

Champion (New Franken), Wisconsin
United States
1859

THE FIRST APPARITIONS TO BE APPROVED IN THE UNITED STATES

THE declaration of approval for the first apparitions to be approved in the United States took place on the Feast of the Immaculate Conception, December 8, 2010, when Bishop L. Ricken of Green Bay formally announced that the appearances of the Blessed Mother to Adele Brise in 1859, were authentic. Before a huge crowd in the shrine of Our Lady of Good Help, Bishop Ricken gave this welcome news:

> I declare with moral certainty and in accord with the norms of the Church that the events, apparitions and locutions given Adele Brise in 1859 do exhibit the substance of supernatural character, and I do hereby approve these apparitions as worthy of belief (although not obligatory) by the Christian faithful.

The bishop's decision to affirm the apparitions took place only after he received a favorable decision from three theologians who had been appointed by him two years earlier. They studied the nature and history of the appearances, the character of the visionary, and the many miracles and answers to prayer that resulted.

ADELE BRISE, A BELGIAN IMMIGRANT TO THE UNITED STATES

According to the shrine in Wisconsin, the history of the apparitions begins with a Belgian immigrant to the United States, Adele Brise, who was born in Dion-le-Val on January 30, 1831. A healthy and energetic child, Adele was unfortunately involved in an accident with lye that caused blindness in one eye. She endured this handicap patiently and was known for her charming personality and religious fervor. Although burdened with a meager education, she had a fervent desire to become a religious in her homeland, but when her parents were making preparations to leave for the United States, she sought the advice of her confessor. He told her that she might still become a religious in the new country, so she accepted his advice. Together with her parents, Lambert and Marie Catherine Brise, and three siblings, the twenty-four-year-old Adele left Belgium in early June of 1855. After enduring all the hardships of a seven-week voyage, they arrived safely in New York.

From there they journeyed west and settled on the Green Bay Peninsula where they established a farm on 240 acres of land they had purchased for $120.00. Adele settled into the routine of daily chores, one of which led to an encounter with the Mother of God.

THE FIRST APPARITION

The apparition was recorded for us by Sister Pauline LaPlant to whom Adele told her story:

> Adele was going to the grist mill about four miles from Champion with a sack of wheat on her head. As Adele came near the place, she saw a lady all in

white standing between two trees, one a maple, the other a hemlock. Adele was frightened and stood still. The vision slowly disappeared, leaving a white cloud after it. Adele continued on her errand and returned home without seeing anything more. She told her parents what had happened, and they wondered what it could be—perhaps a poor soul who needed prayers?

THE SECOND APPARITION

Sister Pauline's testimony continued:

On the following Sunday, October 9, 1859, Adele had to pass there again on her way to Mass at the Bay Settlement, about eleven miles from her home. This time she was not alone, but was accompanied by her sister, Isabel, and a neighbor woman, Mrs. Vander Niessen. When they approached the trees, the same lady in white was standing where Adele had seen her before. Adele was again frightened and said, almost in a tone of reproach, "Oh, there is that lady again."

Adele had not the courage to go on. The other two did not see anything, but they could tell by Adele's look that she was afraid. They thought, too, that it might be a poor soul who needed prayers. They waited a few minutes, until Adele told them it was gone. The vision had disappeared as during the first time, and all Adele could see remaining was a little mist or white cloud. After Mass, Adele went to confession and told her confessor how she had been frightened at the sight of a lady in white. Father William Verhoef bade her not to fear, and to speak to him of this outside the confessional. Father

Verhoef told her that if it were a heavenly messenger, she would see it again, and it would not harm her, but to ask in God's name who it was and what it desired of her. After that, Adele had more courage. She started home with her two companions and a man who had been clearing land for the Holy Cross Fathers.

THE THIRD APPARITION

That same day,

As they approached the hallowed spot (October 9, 1859), Adele could see the beautiful Lady clothed in dazzling white, with a yellow sash around her waist. Her dress fell to her feet in graceful folds. She had a crown of stars around her head, and her long, golden, wavy hair fell loosely around her shoulders. Such a heavenly light shone around her that Adele could hardly look back at her sweet face. Overcome by this heavenly light and the beauty of her amiable visitor, Adele fell on her knees and asked, "In God's name who are you and what do you want of me?" The beautiful Lady responded,

"I am the Queen of Heaven, who prays for the conversion of sinners, and I wish you to do the same. You received Holy Communion this morning, and that is well. But you must do more. Make a general confession, and offer Communion for the conversion of sinners. If they do not convert and do penance, my Son will be obliged to punish them."

When one of Adele's companions asked Adele, "Who is it and why can't we see her as you do?" Adele said, "Kneel. The Lady says she is the Queen of Heaven." The Blessed Mother turned, looked at the companions and said, "Blessed are they that believe without seeing." Then looking at Adele she asked, "What are you doing here in idleness . . . while your companions are working in the vineyard of my son?"

"What more can I do, dear Lady?" Adele asked while shedding heartfelt tears. "How shall I teach them who know so little myself?"

The radiant visitor instructed, "Teach them their catechism, how to sign themselves with the Sign of the Cross, and how to approach the sacraments; that is what I wish you to do. Go and fear nothing. I will help you."

After the Lady lifted her hands as though beseeching a blessing for those at her feet, she slowly vanished, leaving Adele prostrate on the ground.

Although some scoffed at the report of Adele and the vision, her father believed and honored the apparition by erecting a small ten-by-twelve-foot chapel near the place of her vision.

Soon after the great event, Adele obeyed the directive given by the Blessed Mother. She began catechizing children and correcting sinners throughout the area. So effective were her efforts that the Reverend Philip Crud in 1865 advised her to solicit funds for the building of a convent and to recruit help from pious women. Shortly afterward a group of Franciscan tertiaries, with Adele as their superior, began to assist Adele in all her endeavors. These devoted women helped Adele in soliciting funds and with Adele, they were often obliged to ask local farmers for produce, grain and meat to feed the students and her little community.

While Church authorities rejected Adele's efforts, she was nevertheless joined by many who resorted to prayer for the humble shrine's acceptance and success. Soon miracles were taking place; cures of the blind and lame. But the most spectacular miracle took place on October 9 and 10, 1871, the anniversary of Adele's third apparition.

THE FOURTH APPARITION

The miracle involved a fire, now known as the Peshtigo Fire, which began and quickly spread through 400 square miles of northeastern Wisconsin, killing about 1,500 people. It soon spread to the Belgian region. Many, fearing the flames, fled to the lake for refuge while Adele and her community called upon Heaven for protection. To demonstrate their confidence in the Blessed Virgin, they removed her statue from the chapel and carried it in procession around the perimeter of the land together with all the people who had come there for protection. This was to be the first of many processions. When the fire was extinguished, it was seen that the fire had destroyed all the land outside the chapel grounds and had stopped abruptly at the fence. It had miraculously left undisturbed the five acres of the shrine and all the cattle and farm animals which had been brought there for safety.

All seems to have gone well for Sister Adele until one day when she was on her way to Mass. She was thrown from a wagon, and experienced constant physical pain from that time until her death. Unable to continue the management of the school because of her painful condition, the care of the school was passed to another. One day Sister Adele spoke the words, "I rejoiced in what was said to me. We shall go into the house of the Lord." She died that day, July 5, 1896, and was laid to rest in the little cemetery near the chapel. Sister Adele was sixty-six years of age.

ANOTHER CHAPEL IS BUILT

The simple chapel built by Adele's father soon after the apparition, quickly became inadequate for the many people who visited. Another chapel was built when Gregory and Isabella Doyen donated the five acres of land that encompassed the site of the apparitions. One wooden chapel replaced another until a chapel of brick was constructed, which received the blessing of Bishop Krautbauer in October 1880. One of the former students of Adele's school recalls the building of the 1880 chapel:

> I remember well, when I was about eight years old, we would pray and sing hymns around the trees where the Virgin Mother had appeared to Sister Adele. I also remember when the brick chapel was built and the precious trees were cut down to build the chapel, and the altar placed on the spot.

There are carefully preserved remnants of the trees, as well as other precious relics kept in the chapel.

The work this good sister started continues. The simple chapel and school have been enlarged and improved during the years, and today beautiful brick buildings house a convent and school, a chapel with a crypt that was dedicated in July 1942. The crypt and altar that stand over the place of the apparitions have behind them a number of crutches that represent the many miracles that happened at the shrine. An outdoor Way of the Cross and a Rosary walk are available to the huge number of pilgrims who continually visit the shrine of Our Lady of Good Help.

In commemoration of the procession that took place during the Peshtigo fire, a procession takes place every August 15, the feast of Our Lady's Assumption. An outdoor Holy Mass is offered for the thousands in attendance.

One of the sisters who worked with Sister Adele left us this little memorial of her:

Sister had a great deal to suffer from some misun-
derstandings, especially from the clergy; but all this
was to make her feel that this is not our true home,
and she took it in good faith. I never heard her say
an unkind word against them. She was always chari-
table and obedient. Her work prospered, and she
did a great deal of good. Dear Sister Adele, from
your happy home above, remember us.

More than a hundred years after her death, pilgrims by the
thousands visit the shrine where prayers are answered, many are
converted and miracles of healing are granted. It is apparent to
all that the good sister's work continues to prosper as the Mother
of God knew it would.

OUR LADY OF HOPE

Pontmain, France
1871

OUR Blessed Mother, in all her extraordinary apparitions, has consoled, instructed, warned and protected her children. So it was in 1871, when protection was needed for the small village of Pontmain. Nearby, the little town of Laval, the chief town of the department of Mayenne, was expected to receive the Prussians' next attack. After Laval, Pontmain would be taken with no trouble. Paris was already besieged by Prussian forces and war-torn France was in complete disarray. It was a precarious time for its people, but the situation would change dramatically after the apparition of the Blessed Virgin.

THE FIRST PHASE OF THE APPARITION

It was about six o'clock in the evening, when two little brothers, Eugene aged twelve, and Joseph Barbadette aged ten, were working in their father's barn. Eugene decided to see what the weather was like, walked to the door and looked out. Across the way, under a star-studded sky, he noticed something in the air above a neighbor's house. Suddenly he saw a beautiful Lady smiling at him. Although their father, who was in the barn, did not see anything, his brother Joseph also saw the same apparition, a beautiful woman wearing a long blue gown strewn with golden stars. The evening was clear and bright and there was no mistaking what they saw even though their mother also did not see the apparition. Forced to enter the house for the evening meal, the boys ate hastily, rushed out and again saw the beautiful Lady.

Joseph Barbadette, who later became a priest of the Congregation of the Oblates of Mary Immaculate, described the vision as follows:

> In the air above Augustin Guidecoq's house, I saw a woman of extraordinary beauty. She appeared to be young, about eighteen or twenty years of age, and tall of stature. She was clad in a garment of deep blue. When we were told to describe exactly the shade of this blue, we could only do so by comparing it to balls of indigo such as laundresses use for rinsing linen. Her dress was covered with golden stars, pentagonal in form, all of the same size, and brilliant, but without emitting rays. They were not very numerous, and seemed to be scattered over the blue without regard to method. The blue garment was ample, showing certain strongly marked folds, and without girdle or compression of any kind from neck to the feet. The sleeves were ample and long, falling over the hands. On the feet, which the dress left uncovered, were *chaussons* (shoes), the same blue as the dress, and ornamented with golden bows. On the head was a black veil half covering the forehead, concealing the hair and ears, and falling over the shoulders. Above this was a gold crown resembling a diadem, higher in front than elsewhere and widening out at the sides. A red line encircled the crown at about the middle. The hands were small and extended toward us as in the "miraculous medal," but without emitting rays. The face was slightly oval. To the freshness of youth was added the most

exquisite delicacy of feature and of tint, the com-
plexion being pale rather than otherwise. Smiles of
ineffable sweetness played about the mouth. The
eyes, of unutterable tenderness, were fixed on us. I
give up further attempting to describe the beautiful
figure of her who looked down upon us and smiled.
Like a true mother, she seemed happier in looking
at us than we in contemplating her.

Others were alerted to the vision and two little girls who
were brought forth, Françoise Richer and Jeanne-Marie Lebrosse
also saw the apparition, but another little girl did not. The sisters
of the school were notified and also Father Guerin, the pastor
of Pontmain. They, together with about sixty villagers gathered
before the barn and knelt in the snow to begin praying. Sister
Mary Edward began leading in the recitation of the Rosary.
Afterward, Father Guerin led in singing hymns and reciting
other prayers. The Lady became more beautiful and her garments more intense in proportion to the devotion of the people.
The Blessed Mother was actually seen in five phases in which
one scene is taken away to be replaced by another.

THE SECOND PHASE

While the children looked on with amazement, the vision
began to change to the second phase. They watched intently as a
blue oval, darker than the Virgin's dress, began forming around
the figure. Four candles appeared inside the oval, two on either
side of the Virgin's shoulders, the other two on either side about
the height of the knees. A small red heart appeared on the left
chest which was to stay for the remainder of the vision. The stars
on the gown of the Virgin remained while others outside the
oval arranged themselves beneath the Virgin's feet. These stars,
about forty in number, were visible only to the children, but a

triangle of three stars was seen by the villagers. After a moment, the children said, "Oh, there are so many stars the Blessed Virgin will soon be gilt all over."

The children reported during the recitation of the Rosary that Our Lady continued smiling and appeared as a perfectly living creature. When the Holy Mother smiled at her children, they saw her teeth, which were of dazzling whiteness. As soon as the Rosary was finished, Sister Mary Edward began the *Magnificat*. The four children then cried out that something was about to happen.

A white band, about one yard wide, extended across the roof of Guidecoq's house and unrolled itself. On it appeared letters which read, "*Mais priez, mes enfants.*" (But pray, my children.)

The *Magnificat* was still being sung when Joseph Babin, a workman of the village, announced the dreadful news that the Prussians were at nearby Laval. The singing continued as more letters appeared on the white band: "*Dieu vous exaucera en peu de temps*" (God will hear you in a little while). Then more words formed, "*Mon fils se laisse toucher*" (My Son permits Himself to be moved). All those present were overjoyed at hearing the words promising safety from the threat of violence that seemed imminent.

THE THIRD PHASE

The third phase began when the villagers started singing a hymn of the region,

> Mother of Hope, whose name is so sweet,
> protect our land of France,
> Pray, pray for us.

While this was being sung, the Virgin assumed an expression of extreme sadness. Then a blue band, the color of the sky, passed over the blessed words on the white band and effaced them. The banner started rolling away while the Virgin lifted her hand to the level of her shoulders and seemed to move her fingers and speak, but nothing was heard.

THE FOURTH PHASE

The fourth phase began when the vision joined both hands and held upon her heart a red cross with a red image of her crucified Son. A small white sign above the cross read "Jesus Christ." A star then appeared from beneath the Virgin's feet, rose to light the two candles on the Virgin's right side and moved around the top of the oval to light the candles on the left. It then took a position above the vision's head. The crowd then sang the *Ave Maris Stella* and while so doing, the red crucifix disappeared, while the vision assumed the attitude of the apparition of the Immaculate Conception. On each of her shoulders appeared a small white cross about eight inches high.

THE FIFTH PHASE

The fifth phase began when the priest started the recitation of evening prayers. When they reached the examination of conscience, the vision smiled and the cross disappeared. The vision opened her arms as is seen on the Miraculous Medal, and a white veil appeared at her feet and rose slowly upward until the Lady was completely concealed by it. The vision was over. It had lasted three hours.

It was then about nine o'clock, and the crowd that had formed was disappointed that the vision was over but was soon overjoyed when they learned that the Prussian General Schmidt announced to the troops in Laval during the time of the apparition, "We can go no farther, an invisible Madonna is barring the way." The army retreated and twelve days later the armistice was signed. The Heavenly Mother had defended her children.

Ecclesiastical authority, after thoroughly inspecting the reports of the vision, fully approved the apparition in February 1875. A large basilica was built at Pontmain and consecrated in 1900.

Religious life seemed destined for three of the four visionaries. Joseph Barbadette became a priest, a member of the Congregation of the Oblates of Mary Immaculate, while his brother Eugene became a priest of the archdiocese. Françoise Richer became a housekeeper for a priest while Jeanne-Marie Lebosse became a nun.

The apparition was defined by Bishop Laval in February 1875, by declaring: "We judge that the Immaculate Mary, Mother of God, has truly appeared on January 17, 1871, to Eugene Barbadette, Joseph Barbadette, Françoise Richer, and Jeanne-Marie Lebosse, in the hamlet of Pontmain."

Our Lady of St. Bauzille-de-la-Sylve

Hérault, France
1873

AUGUSTE Arnaud was a good man, thirty years of age, who regularly attended Holy Mass on Sundays. He had been married six years, was the father of two children and a respected member in his community. But he was accustomed to doing something that the Blessed Mother did not like, and she meant to correct him. What the Virgin did not like was that Auguste worked on Sundays.

THE FIRST VISION

According to custom, Auguste attended Holy Mass on Sunday, June 8, 1873, the Feast of the Holy Trinity, and then went to his vineyard to tend the vines. After working two hours, Auguste sat down to rest, eat his packaged lunch and smoke his pipe. While doing this, he suddenly saw before him a beautiful young woman dressed in white. He described the vision as wearing a white veil that reached to her feet. She wore a fringed belt and a tall crown like those worn by bishops.

Auguste quickly rose to his feet and asked, "Who are you?"

The vision replied, "I am the Blessed Virgin. Do not be afraid."

Auguste was reassured by these words and listened with great emotion as Mary continued to speak:

> You have the disease of the vine. You left St.
> Bauzille. We must celebrate his feast on the day it
> falls. Next Thursday you must go in procession to
> St. Anthony and hear Mass. In a fortnight you must
> go in procession to Notre-Dame, to the Canton of
> Gignac, Montpellier and the city of Lodeve. You
> must place a cross here, changing it later to another.
> Come in procession each year. Go tell your father
> and your pastor all of this. In a month I will come
> to thank you.

After these words, the apparition rose vertically and gradually disappeared.

Auguste left the vineyard immediately, and on arriving home he excitedly told his father what he had seen. Together they went to the village priest to tell him, but the priest met their remarks with coldness and skepticism, asking, "Why would the Madonna appear to tell a man not to work on Sundays?"

Nevertheless, Auguste continued to perform the mission given him by the beautiful Lady. The next day he contacted a carpenter who crafted a cross made of wood. Auguste took it to the vineyard and planted it where the Blessed Mother had indicated. It was only a temporary one since, according to the Virgin, he was to replace it with a wrought iron cross with the image of the Virgin in the middle.

On June 12, he and his family visited the chapel of St. Anthony, and on June 22 he made the pilgrimage to Our Lady of Grace in Gignac and the other places requested by the Lady. Finally, on July 4, he replaced the wooden cross with an iron cross that he set on a stone pedestal.

THE SECOND VISION

News of the vision spread everywhere so that many of the curious and the skeptics journeyed to the vineyard to witness the second vision promised by the Lady.

Expecting a large crowd, Auguste's wife was very concerned and wondered what would happen to him if the Lady did not appear, and the people, who had traveled from far away, were disappointed. But Auguste did not fear and fully expected the Lady to come as she had predicted.

On the day promised, July 8, 1873, Auguste and a crowd numbering about five hundred people went to the vineyard to await the time of the apparition. After a few moments, Auguste took off his hat and raised both arms high in the air and seemed transfixed by what he saw. But the people saw nothing.

In a moment or two with his arms still raised, Auguste was carried with uncommon speed to the cross about forty yards away. He prayed silently while looking at the Virgin who was dressed in the same manner as before except that now her clothes were colored gold. She held a rosary in her right hand and said sweetly,

> Do not work on Sundays. Blessed is he who believes and unhappy the man who does not believe. You must go to Our Lady of Gignac in procession with your whole family.

She slipped the rosary to her left hand and raising her right hand high, she blessed Auguste and the crowd.

She spoke for the last time before disappearing, "Let us sing hymns."

Auguste turned to the people and in a low voice said, "Tell them to sing." The crowd then began to sing the *Magnificat*.

From that time on, the number of people visiting the area increased so that many candles, flowers, rosaries and ex-votos were collected. This piqued the interest of the bishop who promptly appointed a Commission of Inquiry. After witnesses were questioned, and the work of the commission was completed, the bishop, in 1876, recognized the authenticity of the apparitions.

A chapel, as well as a convent for Franciscan nuns, was built near the place of the visitation. For many years the nuns cared for the sanctuary and the people who visited there.

Auguste Arnaud died on February 8, 1936, at the age of ninety-two, and was buried in the chapel where his tomb reads:

> At the feet of the Virgin he so loved and so faithfully
> served, here lies in wait for the blessed resurrection
> the body of Augustus Arnaud, piously asleep in the
> Lord's peace.

Our Lady of Pellevoisin

Pellevoisin, France
1876

STELLE Faguette, aged thirty-three, lay dying of pulmonary tuberculosis, an abdominal tumor, and acute peritonitis and was expected to live only a few hours, when she experienced an apparition the night of February 14 to 15.

THE FIRST VISION

That night a devil appeared at the foot of her bed to harass her during her final hours, but almost immediately she saw the Blessed Mother at her bedside. The Lady rebuked the devil who departed instantly. Then the Virgin looked at Estelle and told her not to fear, that she would suffer five more days in honor of the five wounds of Christ, and that in a few days, she would be either dead or cured. Estelle would experience fifteen visits from the Mother of God.

THE SECOND VISION

When Our Lady presented herself for the second visit the night of February 15 to 16, it was again after the devil first appeared. The Lady encouraged Estelle,

> Be not afraid, for I am here. My Son is again show-
> ing His mercy. You will be healed on Saturday, but
> you will not be free from troubles or suffering. This
> is what life brings. My Son's heart was pleased by
> your self-denial and patience.

ESTELLE'S FAULTS REVEALED BY THE
BLESSED VIRGIN

After a few moments, the Lady smiled and said, "Now let us
look at your past." When her faults were revealed, Estelle said,
"I was completely stunned by the number of them and remained
silent." The Virgin gently reprimanded her, and then, with an
expression of love, she disappeared.

During the third nighttime visit of February 16 to 17, the
devil once more presented himself but went away as soon as the
Virgin appeared. Estelle, shamed by the faults that were revealed
to her the night before, hung her head, but the Lady told her:
"That is all past, by your self-denial you have put all things
right." The Lady then explained:

> The few good works and the intense prayers that
> you offered me have touched my Motherly heart.
> Do not lose the graces you have been given and
> make my glory known.

In the fourth visitation of February 17 to 18, the Lady cautioned, "Do not be afraid of anything . . . Have courage, patience
and resignation. You will suffer and will be troubled. Try to be
faithful and make my glory known."

During the night of the fifth vision, February 18 to 19, the
Blessed Mother recommended: "If you want to serve me, be
simple and let your deeds prove your words." Then very quietly,

> It saddens me the most to see that people have no
> respect for my Son in the Holy Eucharist and the
> way the people pray while their minds are distracted
> with other matters. I say this to those who pretend
> to be pious.

For the seventh visit of July 2, while Estelle was praying the Rosary beside her bed, the Blessed Virgin appeared in a bright light that was streaming from her hands. She crossed her hands over her chest and said, "You have already proclaimed my glory." She then entrusted Estelle with a secret.

For the ninth apparition, on September 9, the Virgin was concerned with the conditions in France and said, "They want to know everything before learning, and understand everything before knowing . . ."

The Lady was distraught during the eleventh apparition on September 15, and said emphatically, "France will suffer . . . I can stop my Son no longer . . . they will acknowledge the truth of my warning later on."

The twelfth visit was memorable in that the Blessed Mother appeared wearing a scapular that she wanted Estelle to make and promote. On the front was a red heart encircled with thorns, with flaming tongues of fire on top and with blood spilling from a wound on its side. On the reverse was depicted the Lady of Pellevoisin with graces flowing from her hands and framed in an oval of flowers. For the fourteenth vision on November 11, the Lady once again wore the scapular and asked Estelle how many she had sewn. On learning the number, the Lady said, "You must make many more."

The fifteenth and final apparition took place on December 8, the feast of the Immaculate Conception. Estelle was very eager to see the Lady, but also sad that it would be the last time. Estelle relates that the Virgin was more beautiful than before, that she wore a long dress and a floor-length veil and was again wearing

the scapular she had designed. After a moment of silence, the
Lady revealed,

> I am totally merciful and the mistress of my Son
> . . . He will touch the most hardened hearts for me.
> I have especially come to save sinners. The treasures
> of my Son have been open wide for a long time, if
> only they would pray.

Then, while pointing to the scapular she added, "I love this
devotion. I implore all to come to rest and peace . . . Also the
Church and France."

Moved with deep devotion, Estelle asked if she might kiss
the scapular worn by the Blessed Mother. The Lady agreed and
held it forward to receive Estelle's sign of veneration. The Blessed
Mother then instructed Estelle to contact her pastor and the
bishop concerning the propagation of the scapular. The Virgin
opened her hands and graces fell from them in the form of rain,
but on each drop appeared a word: health, trust, respect, love,
holiness and words denoting other graces. The Lady then said:
"These graces are from my Son. I take them out of His heart. He
can refuse me nothing." After a moment, the Lady disappeared.

The apparitions were quickly recognized by Msgr. de La
Tour d'Auvergne, the Archbishop of Bourges, when he authorized the making and distribution of the scapular and allowed
public worship of Our Lady of Pellevoisin. The Archbishop
ordered two canonical inquiries into the apparitions, which
resulted in a favorable verdict on December 5, 1878. Later, in
1883, the parish priest of Pellevoisin, Fr. Salmon, accompanied
by Fr. Auvrelle, the Vicar General, journeyed to Rome to present Pope Leo XIII with a bound record of the apparitions and
a picture of Our Lady of Pellevoisin. The Pope was pleased to
grant indulgences to encourage pilgrimages to the shrine and
also approved the Archconfraternity of Our Mother All Merci-
ful of Pellevoisin.

APPROVAL OF THE SCAPULAR

Estelle was privileged to visit Pope Leo XIII on two occasions, during which the Pope promised to submit her scapular of the Sacred Heart to the Congregation of Rites. Two months later, a decree was issued which granted approval of the scapular.

The miraculous recovery of Estelle during the first apparition was given official and public recognition by Archbishop Paul Vignacour, Archbishop of Bourges, in 1983, following both medical and theological investigations.

Estelle Faguette, a privileged soul, died in Pellevoisin, on August 23, 1929, at the age of eighty-six.

THE VIRGIN MARY OF THE
IMMACULATE CONCEPTION

Gietrzwald, Poland
1877

NINETEEN years after the apparitions at Lourdes in which the Blessed Mother identified herself as the Immaculate Conception, she called herself by the same name to two indigent girls in Gietrzward, Poland. The visionaries were Justyna Szafrynska who was thirteen years old and Barbara Samulowska who was twelve.

THE FIRST APPARITION

Justyna had just taken an examination prior to receiving her First Holy Communion and was walking home with her mother when she saw the Blessed Mother in front of the church in Gietrzwald. The date was June 27, 1877. The next day Barbara also saw the "bright lady" sitting on a throne with the Infant Jesus. The vision, which was surrounded by angels, took place near a maple tree in front of the parish church.

Both girls asked the Blessed Mother, "What do you require, Mother of God?" The heavenly answer was "I would like you to recite the Rosary every day." As to the question, "Who are you?" The vision answered, "I am the Blessed Virgin Mary of the Immaculate Conception."

The girls asked other questions, including whether sick people who came there would be healed. The vision assured them that many would be healed, but they should pray the Rosary.

THE SECOND APPARITION

Because the area was then under the oppression of the Russians, Barbara asked the apparition on August 1, 1877, during the second apparition, whether the deserted parishes would open and receive priests. The Holy Mother answered, "If people pray zealously the Church will not be persecuted and the parishes will receive their priests."

On August 8, at seven o'clock in the evening, the Holy Mother blessed the nearby spring and said the words: "Now the sick people can take this water for their healing." The water from this spring has been used as a sacramental ever since.

The Blessed Mother appeared for the last time on September 16, 1877.

Our Lady's predictions had come true. Many were healed by using the water from the spring, and the closed parishes were opened with many priests assigned to them.

Before the last of the visions, the administrator of the diocese, Bishop Filip Krementz, assembled a commission to examine the authenticity of the apparitions. The members were to observe the state and behavior of the visionaries in the course of their apparitions and to prepare a record of their testimonies and those of pilgrims and clergy.

The commission's first declaration was that the girls behaved normally and did not seem to be seeking profit or acknowledgment. "They possessed modesty, sincerity and simplicity."

After receiving the results of the commission, the bishop promoted the publication in German and Polish of a study entitled "The Apparitions of Our Lady in Gietrzw"ard to the

Catholic People According to the Official Documents."

As in all churches in the world, the Gietrzward church also has a revered image, a portrait of the Blessed Madonna holding the Infant Jesus on her left arm. In time, the garments and crowns were sheathed in silver. Dating from 1568, the portrait was renovated many times. For the ninetieth anniversary of the apparitions the Primate of Poland, Cardinal Stefan Wyszynski visited the shrine and crowned the image. Soon after, the Holy See granted the Gietrzward Virgin's feast to be observed on September 8 with special propers (the prayers that pertain specifically to the feast being celebrated) of the Mass and Breviary. Pope Paul VI elevated the church in Gietrzward to the rank of Basilica Minor.

The apparitions were again confirmed on the one hundredth anniversary by Bishop Jozef Drzazga and reads in part,

> Taking into account the conformity of the Gietrzward apparitions with faith and morality, the integrity of the recipients of those apparitions, and the blest effects of them over the whole century . . . we hereby approve the devotion to Our Lady's apparitions in Gietrzward as not contradicting Christian faith and morality whose miraculous and divine nature cannot be excluded.

As a result of the visions, the people took Our Lady's message to heart and recited the Rosary in private homes, in churches, and in groups. In some churches, the Rosary was recited three times a day.

The visionaries received their education in the St. Joseph House in Pelplin. Both took the habit of the Sisters of Charity in 1880. Barbara Samulowska was in France for a time and was then sent to Guatemala where she was the administrator of the Central Hospital for many years.

Our Lady of Knock

Knock, County Mayo, Ireland
1879

THE history of the Irish nation in the mid-nineteenth century reveals a time of cruel hardship for the people, with famines, forced emigrations and tragic deaths from malnutrition. It is said that persons who escaped the hunger were lucky if they were not laid low with disease. There had been a serious failure of the potato crop in 1877 and 1878 to which was added the oppression of landlords and rulers who exacted crushing rents and taxes on the poor. In addition, the Catholic Church was harassed by those who attempted to eliminate Catholic worship by bribing the hungry with food and money to attend Protestant churches. To comfort and sustain the faithful during this time of hardship, the Blessed Mother visited her people in the small hamlet of Knock, located in County Mayo (now known as Cnoc Mhuire). The history of Ireland relates that St. Patrick visited the area and prophesied correctly that it would one day be a place of great devotion.

THE FIRST VISION

It was raining in the quiet village during the twenty-first day of August 1879; a strong wind carried a thick mist against the gable wall of the parish church. In the evening, two women of Knock, Mary McLoughlin and Mary Beirne were walking toward their home when they passed the back of the village church. There, a few feet from the wall, in a radiant light, they saw figures which at first they thought were statues. On closer inspection, Mary Beirne exclaimed, "But they are not statues, they are moving. It's the Blessed Virgin."

They notified others who gathered and gazed in awe at the apparition. On the Blessed Mother's right was St. Joseph, his head inclined toward her. On her left stood St. John the Evangelist, vested as a bishop, his left hand holding a book and his right raised as if preaching. To the left of St. John was an altar on which stood a cross and a lamb, which the people estimated was about eight weeks old. Around the scene were angels moving about. The vision lasted for two hours, during which many of the villagers knelt in prayer before the beautiful, unbelievable scene.

Sometime after the vision, fifteen of the witnesses gave depositions before the archbishop and various dignitaries of the Church. Among the witnesses who were questioned was Patrick Hill. He reported that he was going home about 8 o'clock when he heard of the vision and hurried toward the church.

> I immediately beheld the lights; a clear white light covering most of the gable from the ground up to the window and higher. It was a bright light, going sometimes up high and again not so high. We saw the figures, the Blessed Virgin, St. Joseph and St. John, and an altar with a lamb on the altar and a cross behind the lamb. . . . people were praying, not all were looking at the vision . . . I then went up closer and saw everything distinctly. The figures were full and round as if they had a body and life. They said nothing, but as we approached they seemed to go back a little towards the gable.
>
> I distinctly beheld the Blessed Virgin Mary, life size, standing about two feet or so above the ground

clothed in white robes which were fastened at the neck, her hands were raised to the height of the shoulders as if in prayer, with the palms facing one another and slanting inwards towards the face . . . she appeared to be praying; her eyes were turned as I saw towards Heaven; she wore a brilliant crown on her head and over the forehead where the crown fitted her brow, a beautiful rose; the crown appeared brilliant and of a golden brightness . . . the upper parts of the crown appeared to be a series of sparkles, or glittering crosses. I saw her eyes, the balls, the pupils and the iris of each . . . Her robes came only as far as the ankles; I saw the feet and the ankles; one foot, the right, was slightly in advance of the other. I saw them move, but she did not speak . . . I saw St. Joseph . . . his head was bent and he appeared to be paying his respects to the Blessed Virgin. I noticed his whiskers, they appeared slightly grey. His hands were joined like a person at prayer.

St. John the Evangelist stood erect at the Gospel side of the little altar and at an angle so that his back was not turned to the altar, nor to the Mother of God. He was dressed like a bishop preaching; he wore a small mitre on his head; he held a Mass book in his left hand; the right hand was raised to the elevation of the head while he kept the index finger and the middle finger of the right hand raised, the other three fingers of the same hand were shut. He appeared as if he were preaching, but I heard no voice. I went near and looked into the book he held. I saw the lines and the letters . . . the altar on his left was plain without any ornaments. On it stood a lamb which was facing the west and looking in the direction of the figures . . . I saw angels hovering during the whole time, for the space of one hour and a half or longer; I saw their wings fluttering, but

> I did not perceive their heads or faces which were
> not turned to me. For the space of an hour and a
> half we were under the pouring rain; at this time I
> was very wet; I noticed that the rain did not wet the
> figures . . . I went away then.

His deposition was dated October 8, 1879.

The depositions of the fifteen witnesses agreed on all points regarding the descriptions of the figures and what took place. Mary McLoughlin, however, the housekeeper of the village priest, adds,

> Behind the lamb appeared the cross, it was away a
> bit from the lamb, while the latter stood in front of
> it . . . Around the lamb a number of gold-like stars
> appeared in the form of a halo . . . I parted from the
> gathering at eight and a half o'clock . . . I saw the
> sight for fully an hour."

Mary Beirne says that "the altar had no special ornamentations; it was only a plain altar. Above the altar and resting on it was a lamb . . . On the body of the lamb, and around it, I saw golden stars, or small brilliant lights, glittering like jets or glass balls reflecting the light . . ."

Bridget Trench adds that the figures were raised about two feet above the ground . . .

> it was raining very heavily at the time, but no rain
> fell where the figures were. I felt the ground care-
> fully with my hands and it was perfectly dry . . .
> they appeared to me so full and so lifelike and so
> life-sized that I could not understand why I could
> not feel them with my hands such as I beheld them
> with my eyes . . . I felt great delight and pleasure in
> looking at the Blessed Virgin. I could think of noth-
> ing else while there but giving thanks to God and
> repeating my prayers.

The apparition might be accepted as a reward for the loyalty of the people who suffered distress and afflictions during the hard time of religious persecutions and great privations. But the vision was different from others before and since. The first difference is the number of figures in the apparition. Usually, the Blessed Mother appeared by herself. The second difference is the lack of a verbal message or warning. Again the difference is the large number of people who saw the apparition, and the two-hour length of the vision. Another difference is that this is the first and only vision in which the Lamb of God appears.

Church officials investigated the apparition at Knock in 1879, the year of the apparition, and again in 1936. It was found that the witnesses were believable and that there was nothing contrary to the Faith. Since then, four popes have honored the shrine at Knock. Pope Pius XII blessed the banner of Knock at St. Peter's Basilica and decorated it with a special medal in 1945. Pope John XXIII presented a special candle to Knock on Candlemas Day in 1960. Pope Paul VI blessed the foundation stone for the Basilica of Our Lady of Knock in 1974, and Pope John Paul II made a personal pilgrimage to the shrine on September 30, 1979, to observe the centennial of the apparition. In addition, the shrine was graced by the presence of Mother Teresa of Calcutta who visited the shrine in June 1993. It is estimated that a half million pilgrims visit the shrine annually.*

The shrine is noted for its many cures and divine favors. The first cure occurred only a few days after the apparition when a young girl, born deaf, instantly received the gift of hearing. At the end of 1880, some three hundred cures, deemed miraculous, had been recorded in the diary of the parish priest.

---

* If you would like to visit the shrine it can be done by way of their web page http://www.knock-shrine.ie.

OUR LADY OF SORROWS

Castelpetroso, Italy
1888

NINE years after the apparition in Knock, Ireland, in which the Blessed Mother remained silent, another such vision occurred in Italy during which the Blessed Virgin again said nothing. Just as in Ireland, where many people of the village saw the apparition, so, too, in Castelpetroso crowds of people, including priests and bishops, saw the Heavenly Queen.

THE FIRST VISION

The vision took place on March 22, 1888, the day before the feast of the Compassion of Our Blessed Lady. Two women, Fabiana Cecchino, a thirty-five-year-old unmarried woman and Serafina Giovanna Valentino, a younger married woman, were searching for some lost sheep that had strayed to a neighboring hill, to which Castelpetroso is the nearest village. When they returned home crying, trembling and terrified, they told those who came to help them about the vision they had seen.

They reported that they had seen a light coming through some fissures in a rocky cliff and when they investigated, they saw distinctly the image of Our Lady of Sorrows kneeling beside her deceased Son. She was a fair-skinned, lovely young woman with disheveled hair who was bleeding from seven swords that pierced her heart. This report was met with the expected skepticism, but when a few of the curious visited the place and witnessed the cure of a seriously ill child and the conversion of an avowed heretic, not only did they believe, but so did the crowds that converged there.

A priest of the diocese who for a time disbelieved later saw the apparition and filed this narrative:

> I had many times derided those who visited the mountain on which these wondrous apparitions took place. On May 16, 1888, however, more to pass the time than for anything else, I felt a desire to visit the place. When I arrived I began to look into one of the fissures, and I saw with great clearness Our Lady, like a statuette, with a little Child in her arms. After a short interval I looked again at the same spot; and, in place of the Most Holy Virgin I saw, quite clearly, the dead Saviour bearing the crown of thorns and all covered with blood. From that time forward when I have heard a mention of that thrice-blessed mountain and of the apparition I have felt myself moved to tears, and have not been able to say a word. Signed: Don Luigi Ferrara, Priest.

As at Fatima, in which Our Lady appeared in the sky with the Holy Family and then in the brown robes of Our Lady of Mount Carmel, this vision at Castelpetroso also featured changes in her appearance. Some of the people who climbed the mount of 2,600 feet to the apparition site testified that they saw the Blessed Virgin under the form of Our Lady of Mount Carmel; others saw her as Our Lady of Grace and still others as Our Lady of the Holy Rosary. But the majority saw the vision as Our Lady of Dolors. She was sometimes accompanied by St. Michael, at other times by St. Anthony, St. Sebastian and sometimes by flights of angels.

News of the miracle soon reached Bishop Macarone-Palmieri of the diocese of Bojano in which the village of Castelpetroso is located. On his visit to Rome on other business in September of the same year, he acquainted Pope Leo XIII of the apparitions, and it was the pope's suggestion that an inquiry be conducted and that the bishop should visit Castelpetroso to study the events, which he did on his return. In the company of the archpriest of Bojano, the bishop saw the apparition on three occasions.

During May of 1888, a spring of water appeared at the place of the visions and in March of the following year, the Bishop of Bojano confirmed its existence to the editor of the periodical, *Servo di Maria,* which publicized the fact. Just as the people of Lourdes began to use the water of Bernadette's spring, the people of Castelpetroso began using the water of their new spring for medicinal purposes which resulted in reports of healings and favors received.

The bishop wisely ordered an examination of the evidence and called upon Father Joseph Lais of the Congregation of the Oratory of St. Philip Neri. Father Lais was a physicist, a medical doctor and the sub-director of the Vatican Observatory. Father Lais, in questioning the witnesses, learned that some people saw the apparition on one visit but not on other visits. For instance, one man saw her once in six times, another might have seen nothing, while another had seen Our Lady on almost every visit. According to a reliable source, the apparition was so overwhelming that two men fainted.

After carefully examining all aspects of the visions and reported cures, this well-appointed scientist declared without reservation that the apparitions were not the result of optical delusion and that any claim otherwise was ill founded. Father Lais declared in a statement:

> The observations I made of the character of the people lead me to recognize that they are profoundly

convinced of the event having taken place; and, on the other hand, their simple and ingenuous demeanor does not suggest the suspicion that the fact should be, to some extent, fanciful or the effect of the imagination; whilst the natural formation of the rocks excludes the theory of trickery.

After this favorable report, the Bishop of Bojano formed a committee for the purpose of planning the collection of funds for a church to be built on the place favored by the Blessed Mother. In approval of this effort, Pope Leo XIII had his Secretary of State, Cardinal Rampolla, send a message imparting the Apostolic Blessing to the members of the committee and to all those who contributed to the fund. In May of 1890, the cornerstone was laid for a beautiful Gothic church.

In a lengthy article published in 1888 by the religious periodical, *Servo di Maria,* the Bishop of Bojano gives details of the apparition, which includes his own experience.

I myself can bear witness that I visited the sacred spot, and after sometime spent in prayer, saw the apparition of the Blessed Virgin. At first the image of Our Lady appeared faint and indistinct, but at length she appeared in the attitude and proportions of the representation of the Mother of Sorrows . . . Beside myself and the very large number of persons whose names are recorded in the official report, there are the Vicar General of the Diocese, the Archpriest of the Cathedral, and many other ecclesiastics who also beheld the miraculous apparitions . . .

In March of 1995, a special celebration was observed by the Supreme Pontiff, Pope John Paul II, who went as a pilgrim to Castelpetroso. With crowds of people waving the papal flag, the pope arrived in an open car and reached the precincts of the sanctuary accompanied by His Excellency, Monsignor Ettore Di

Filippo, Archbishop of Campobasso-Bojano. After a special salutation to the sick, the Holy Father entered the sanctuary where for several minutes he remained recollected in prayer before the statue of the Sorrowful Mother.

OUR LADY OF CHINA

Dong Lu, China
1900 and 1995

BOXER REBELLION

*T*HE anti-colonialist, anti-Christian members of the Boxer Rebellion harassed China between November 2, 1899, and September 7, 1901. They were against many political issues, but were also against religion and often attacked mission compounds. They also besieged foreign embassies and performed so many atrocities that diplomats, foreign civilians, soldiers and some Chinese Christians retreated to the Legation Quarter where they stayed fifty-five days until the Eight-nation Alliance, which included the United States, brought twenty thousand armed troops to defeat the rebels.

THE FIRST APPARITION

But during the time of their activity, in the year 1900, ten thousand rebels attacked the small impoverished village of Dong Lu, the home of about one thousand Christians. While firing their weapons into huddled groups of frightened Christians, the attackers suddenly began shooting in the air. When they saw that their attack was not gaining the expected result, they stopped. It was then that the people saw in the air a vision of the Blessed Virgin surrounded by a mystical light. The rebels, to their surprise and shock, were chased from the village by the apparition of a fiery horseman thought to have been St. Michael.

Grateful for Our Lady's protection, the villagers built a beautiful church in her honor. The pastor at the time had a painting made that depicted the Virgin dressed in the imperial robes of Dowager Empress XI, and the Christ Child clothed in a costly imperial robe. This painting was hung in the church of Dong Lu where it was honored by pilgrimages starting in 1924. It was this painting that was officially sanctioned in the name of Our Lady of China. It was blessed by Pope Pius XI in 1928, in response to the requests made by the 1924 Shanghai Synod of Bishops in China. This was the first national conference of bishops in the country.

The little church was recognized in 1932, when Pope Pius XI approved the church as an official Marian Shrine. Pope Pius XII in 1941 designated the second Sunday of May as a special feast day of Our Lady of China and approved its insertion in the liturgical calendar.

Unfortunately, the little shrine was destroyed during the Second World War when the Japanese bombed it, but it was rebuilt in 1992, and is now the largest church in Northern China.

THE SECOND APPARITION

Yet another apparition of Our Lady and Christ Child took place on May 23, 1995, when 30,000 Catholics gathered at the shrine on the vigil of the Feast of Our Lady, Mary Help of Christians. Present were four bishops and almost one hundred priests who gathered in an open field to celebrate an outdoor Holy Mass. When the opening prayer began, and then again during the Consecration, everyone observed the sun spinning from right to left with various colors emanating from it. Our

Lady of China holding the Child Jesus was also clearly seen. Just as at Fatima, during the miracle of the sun, when the tableau increased, here too Our Lady was met by the Holy Family and other figures. The phenomenon lasted approximately twenty minutes.

PILGRIMS FORBIDDEN ACCESS TO THE CHURCH

The following day, May 24, 1995, members of the Public Security Forces forbade pilgrims to gather on the hill and forced many into buses and trains. An estimated one hundred thousand, however, went by way of different routes and successfully joined others to celebrate the Feast of Mary, Our Lady of China.

The harassment of pilgrims continued the next year when, in April and May 1996, five thousand troops were mobilized with thirty armored cars and helicopters in an effort to isolate the village. At this time a dearly loved statue of Mary was confiscated. The painted portrait of the Blessed Mother and Child was saved because it had been safely hidden while a reproduction was displayed in the church. The original portrait is in the possession of Chinese priests who carry out their activities in disguise.

Presently, because of the political situation in China, many bishops, priests and Catholics, loyal to the Pope, have been arrested and tortured. Pilgrimages to Dong Lu have been declared illegal by the government, and the faithful who are loyal to the Pope must observe services in secret. There is an "official church" in which certain services are permitted, and these are strictly monitored by the government.

Every year on October 1, celebrations are held that commemorate Pope John Paul II's canonization of the 120 martyrs of the Boxer Rebellion.

OUR LADY OF FATIMA

Fatima, Portugal
1917

THE THREE VISIONARIES AT FATIMA

THE three visionaries of Fatima, all from the same extended family, include Lucia de Jesus dos Santos, the oldest, who was born on March 22, 1907. She was ten years old when the first apparition of Our Lady took place on May 13, 1917.

Francisco, her cousin, was born on June 11, 1908, the sixth of seven children. He, like his sister Jacinta, was playful, never complained when treated unfairly and was never combative. Francisco never heard the Lady's words, although he saw her and felt her presence.

Jacinta, the third visionary, was two years younger than her brother Francisco. She was a delightful child who loved to dance and collect flowers. Most of all she loved following Lucia to the places where she tended the family's sheep. After the first apparition that included an angel's visit she became very serious and reflective. Jacinta, we are told, was the most generous in complying with Our Lady's wishes to make sacrifices for sinners.

THE ANGEL OF PEACE

During the spring of 1916, the three children, Lucy, Jacinta and Francisco, were playing games as they watched over their family's flock of sheep. Suddenly an angel surrounded by a great light appeared to them and identified himself as The Angel of Peace. He knelt down to demonstrate the fervent manner in which they should pray to God and spoke about the importance of praying and making sacrifices saying:

> Make of everything you can a sacrifice and offer it to God as an act of reparation for the sins by which He is offended, and in supplication, for the conversion of sinners.

In addition, the angel gave the children a prayer, which they piously recited numerous times:

> Most Holy Trinity, Father, Son and Holy Spirit, I adore Thee profoundly. I offer Thee the Most Precious Body, Blood, Soul and Divinity of Jesus Christ, present in all the tabernacles of the world, in reparation for the outrages, sacrileges and indifferences by which He is mortally offended. Through the infinite merits of His Most Sacred Heart and the Immaculate Heart of Mary, I beg the conversion of poor sinners.

During the angel's third and last visit he gave the children Holy Communion. Lucy was given the Sacred Host while the Sacred Blood of Jesus was shared by Francisco and Jacinta.

THE FIRST APPEARANCE OF THE BLESSED MOTHER

The following year, on May 13, 1917, the Blessed Mother appeared to them and encouraged the children to pray the Rosary every day and to practice devotion to her Immaculate Heart "which is so terribly outraged and offended by the sins of men."

The children also realized that God is terribly offended by sins, and that He desires all mankind to abandon sin and make reparation for their crimes through prayer and sacrifices. Our Lady solemnly pleaded, "Do not offend the Lord our God any more, for He is already too much offended!"

During another apparition, the children were briefly shown a vision of Hell after which Our Lady told them,

> You have seen Hell where the souls of poor sinners go. To save them, God wishes to establish in the world devotion to My Immaculate Heart. If what I say to you is done, many souls will be saved and there will be peace.

The Blessed Lady warned that if people did not stop offending God, there would be persecutions of the Church, famine and chastisements.

THE BLESSED MOTHER ASKS FOR THE CONSECRATION OF RUSSIA

During another apparition, she asked for the consecration of Russia to her Immaculate Heart and the Communions of Reparation on the First Saturday of five consecutive months. She also pleaded for the frequent recitation of the Rosary, which she said would obtain for us the graces we need to overcome sin.

"My Immaculate Heart will be your refuge and the way that will lead you to God."

In addition to the Holy Rosary, Our Lady requested sacrifices, including the performance of one's daily duties.

THE LAST APPARITION

The promise of a miracle that would make all the people believe in her appearances took place on October 13, 1917, during the last apparition when thousands of people descended on the Cova de Iria. Since it had rained steadily the night before, the people were thoroughly wet when the time of the predicted miracle was expected. Suddenly their clothes were dry as was the ground that had been saturated. Then the sun began to twirl and emit various lights and appeared to fall towards the earth. When the sun rose to its proper place in the sky, the people were awed by the spectacle and began praying with great emotion and fear.

Two years after the visions, Jacinta and her brother Francisco died as prophesied by the Lady. Both children succumbed to the effects of influenza.

At the age of fourteen, the remaining visionary, Lucia, entered the school conducted by the Sisters of St. Dorothy in Vilar. In 1925, she entered the Order as a postulant. Later, seeking a more contemplative life, Lucia entered the Discalced Carmelite Order in Coimbra on May 13, 1949, taking the name, Sister Mary of the Sorrowful Mother.

In 1930, the bishop of Leiria-Fatima officially declared the apparitions "worthy of credibility." To celebrate the fiftieth anniversary of the apparitions, Pope Paul VI visited the shrine and Pope John Paul II visited three times. In 1982, John Paul II visited and gave thanks for his life being saved during the assassination attempt of May 13, 1981. Another visit was made by him in 1991, and finally in 2000, he went to the basilica at Fatima to beatify Jacinta and Francisco.

The remaining visionary of Fatima, Sister Lucia, died on February 13, 2005, at the age of ninety-seven, and is entombed beside her visionary companions in the basilica at Fatima.

OUR LADY OF VICTORY

Wigratzbad, Germany
1919 and 1938

THE FIRST APPARITION

IN THE year 1919, when Antonie Radler was twenty years old, she contracted the Spanish influenza and was desperately ill. The fervent prayers of her mother persuaded the Blessed Virgin to appear at the patient's bedside. When the apparition laid her hands on the young victim, Antonie was instantly healed.

Fully recovered, Antonie was working one day in her father's butcher shop when the Gestapo arrived and ordered her to replace the painting of the Virgin on the wall with that of the Führer. She was ordered to salute him in the Nazi fashion, saying, "*Heil Hitler*" instead of the usual Bavarian greeting of "*Grüss Gott.*" Antonie refused and barely escaped several attempts on her life. She always maintained that her Guardian Angel, in the form of a mysterious cyclist, protected her.

The parents were so delighted and grateful with her escape from harm that they erected a small Lourdes grotto in their garden. This was blessed by Father Basch, pastor of their parish, on October 11, 1936, the feast day of the Maternity of Mary. The following month, while at prayer before the statue, Antonie saw Mary smile sweetly and heard the words, "O Beloved Lady of Victory, conceived without sin, pray for us."

Then, while praying at the Lourdes grotto on December 15, 1936, during the octave of the Immaculate Conception, and while reciting the third sorrowful mystery of the Rosary, Antonie heard an "angelic chorus" singing, "O Mary! Immaculate, conceived without sin. Beloved Lady of Victory, pray for us."

THE SECOND APPARITION

The history of this appearance of the Blessed Mother at Wigratzbad now shifts to a young girl named Cecilia Geyer who, on February 22, 1938, about half past six in the morning, after hearing a murmur, saw the Blessed Virgin appear in a bright cloud. Cecilia said that suddenly,

> I found myself in the little grotto of Antonie and heard this message, 'Build a chapel here for me. I shall trample underfoot the serpent's head. People will come here in large numbers and I will pour upon them a flood of graces. St. Joseph, St. Anthony and the souls in Purgatory will help you.'"

The Lady then directed, "Go now and worship my Son in the Blessed Sacrament." Realizing that all the churches were closed at that hour, Cecilia asked the vision where should she go? Then, "before my astonished eyes there appeared a chapel in the place designated by the Lady. Inside, on the altar, surrounded by beautiful rays of light was Jesus in a monstrance."

THE BLESSED VIRGIN APPEARS TO ANTONIE IN PRISON

The history of the chapel now reverts to Antonie Radler. Work on the building of a chapel requested by Our Lady was begun on July 2, 1938, on land donated by her parents. All went well until the night of November 21, when Antonie was arrested by the Nazis and incarcerated in the local prison. She underwent numerous interrogations, but on the night of December 7 to 8 she beheld a large cloud arising in her cell. Suddenly the Virgin appeared to her and announced her impending release. She would spend Christmas with the family. Antonie was eventually released on December 18, the Feast of the Expectation of Our Lady.

Today, the chapel built at the sight of the apparitions is host to an estimated five hundred thousand pilgrims each year. Among the visitors in 1991, was Bishop Stimpfle, Archbishop of Augsburg, who assisted at the funeral of Antonie and delivered the funeral oration. No official statement was made by the bishop regarding the apparitions, but he was known to say, "I know that Wigratzbad is authentic!"

THE IMMACULATE HEART OF MARY

Pontevedra, Spain
1925

WHEN the Blessed Mother first appeared at Fatima on May 13, 1917, Lucia, the oldest of the visionaries, was only ten years old. At the age of fourteen, she was admitted as a boarder in the school of the Sisters of St. Dorothy in Vilar. Wanting to dedicate her life to Our Blessed Mother, she entered the Institute of the Sisters of St. Dorothy as a postulant in the convent in Tuy, Spain, on October 24, 1925, and pronounced her perpetual vows on October 3, 1934.

THE FIRST VISION

During her years of religious life she continued to receive messages from Our Blessed Mother, starting on December 10, 1925, while she was still a postulant. In this apparition, Lucia saw the Blessed Mother standing over a cloud of light with the Child Jesus at her side. The Blessed Mother put one hand on Lucia's shoulder while the other hand held her Immaculate Heart that was surrounded with thorns. The Child Jesus spoke, "Have compassion on the Heart of your Blessed Mother. It is surrounded with thorns that ungrateful men pierce each moment and there is no one that is willing to offer an act of reparation to take the thorns away."

The Blessed Virgin then spoke, "Look my daughter. My heart is surrounded with thorns that ungrateful men pierce unceasingly with their blasphemies and ingratitude. You, at least, try to console me. You should announce that I promise for all those who on five consecutive first Saturdays, confess, receive Holy Communion, pray the Holy Rosary with the intention to do reparation, I will assist at the hour of death with the graces needed for salvation."

Our Lord Himself revealed to Lucia the offenses and blasphemies which wound the Immaculate Heart of Mary: those who deny or question the Immaculate Conception, her virginity, her divine maternity and those who instill in children their prejudices against the Immaculate Heart, and those who insult or offend her sacred images.

Our Lord once again appeared to Lucia in February 1926, asking about the promotion of the requests made by His Mother. Lucia could only explain the difficulties she encountered, but Jesus replied that His grace was sufficient.

Another apparition of the Blessed Mother occurred in June 1929. Lucia describes the apparition in this manner:

> suddenly the entire convent chapel was illuminated in a supernatural light, and a cross of light appeared over the altar and reached the ceiling. On the superior part the face of a man was seen and his body down to the waist. A dove of light was over his chest and nailed to the Cross was another man. Suspended in air over his waist I was able to see a chalice with a large Host. Drops of Blood from the face of Jesus Crucified and blood from His pierced side fell into the chalice, dripping from the Host.

Beneath the right arm on the cross was Our Lady who appeared as Our Lady of Fatima. In her left hand was her Immaculate Heart that was encircled by a crown of thorns and flames. Underneath the left arm of the cross, big letters, similar to crystal water came down to the altar forming these words: "Graces and Mercy."

I understood it was the mystery of the Blessed Trinity that was revealed to me, and I perceived inner light about this mystery which I am unable to reveal. The Blessed Virgin told me: "The time has come in which God asks the Holy Father to consecrate Russia to my heart in union with all the bishops of the world. I promise salvation through this means."

In response to Our Lady's request, various consecrations of the world were made by Pope Pius XII, Pope Paul VI and twice by Pope John Paul II. The last consecration by Pope John Paul II in 1984, was considered by Lucia to have been in conformity with the Blessed Mother's request. In the year 2000, Pope John Paul II consecrated the third millennium to the Immaculate Heart of Mary.

In seeking a more contemplative life, Lucia entered the Discalced Carmelite convent of St. Teresa in Coimbra where she made her profession on May 31, 1949. She received the name Sister Maria Lucia of Jesus and the Immaculate Heart.

Sister Lucia wrote two books, *Memoirs*, telling the events of Fatima in her own words, and *Calls from the Message of Fatima*, which answered questions frequently asked of her about the messages of Fatima.

For the fiftieth anniversary of the apparitions at Fatima, Sister Lucia in 1967, traveled there for the ceremonies conducted by Pope Paul VI. When Pope John Paul II visited the Shrine on May 13, 1982, to thank the Immaculate Heart for saving his life during the assassination attempt of May 13, 1981, Sister Lucia was again present. Her last visit to Fatima was in the year 2000, for the beatification of Jacinta and Francisco.

Lucia spent eighty years as a religious and died on February 13, 2005, at the age of ninety-seven, succumbing to the infirmities of old age. Her funeral Mass at the cathedral was presided over by the city's bishop, Most Reverend Antonio Cleto. Her body is now entombed in the basilica in Fatima beside those of Jacinta and Francisco, her companions in the apparitions of Our Lady of Fatima.

Our Lady of Mount Berico. Our Lady appeared to Vicenza Passini in 1426 and 1428, in Vicenza, Italy, which, at the time was suffering from the plague. She requested that a church be built in her honor on Mount Berico. Once the church was finished, the plague disappeared from that area.

Our Lady of Trois-Epis (Three Ears) appeared to Thierry Schoeré in 1491 in Orbey, France, holding three ears of corn in her right hand and a clump of ice in her left. The three ears symbolized the fine harvest that will be reaped by devout souls, while the ice symbolized the punishment that will be dealt to the disbelievers.

Vailankanni Shrine (www.vailankannishrine.org)

Our Lady of Good Health (above) first appeared to a young boy in 1580, on the shore of the Bay of Bengal in India. She asked the boy, who was on his way to sell milk, if she could have some milk for her son. He gave her some and brought what remained to his customer, apologizing that the jar was not full. He and the customer then noticed that the jar had miraculously become full again.

Our Lady of Manaoag (below) appeared in 1610 to a man in Pangasinan, The Philippines, while he was walking home. Our Lady appeared with the Child Jesus in her arms. Later a church was built on the site of the apparition. This church has been miraculously preserved from fire and from bombing during World War II.

Fr. Roland D. Macad, O.P.

Our Lady of Good Success. This image of Our Lady of Good Success originated in Madrid, Spain, but the apparitions of Our Lady to Sr. Mariana de Jesus Torres in Quito, Ecuador, made it better known. Our Lady gave the world many messages and warnings through these apparitions.

Luxemburg

CONSOLATRIX AFFLICTORVM ORA PRO NOBIS

Vera Effigies Matris IESU Consolatricis afflicto-rum in agro suburbano Lvxemburgi Miraculis et Hominum Visitatione celebris, Anno 1640.

Wallfahrtsleitung/Priesterhaus Kevelaer

Comforter of the Afflicted. This image of Our Lady, Comforter of the Afflicted, was miraculously recovered by a tinker and his wife near the town of Weeze, Germany. A shrine was built in its honor and crowds of pilgrims came to venerate it. Many miraculous cures have been attributed to this image.

Our Lady of Laus appeared to Benoite Rencurel in 1664, while she was tending her sheep. She appeared every day for four months and asked Benoite to pray for the conversion of poor sinners. After this she continued to appear in the Laus chapel, where she requested that a larger chapel, and a residence for priests, be built.

Our Lady of Las Lajas. In a cave in the Guaitara Canyon in Colombia, Our Lady appeared to a deaf-mute child named Rosa. Rosa was cured, and this image of Our Lady was discovered on the wall. Scientific testing cannot discover the medium used to make it. The image evenly penetrates into the rock around which a cathedral was built in Our Lady's honor (pictured at right).

Basilica S.Andrea Delle Fratte

Our Lady of the Miracle. Our Lady appeared to Alphonse Ratisbonne in Rome in 1842, after a Catholic friend challenged him to wear the Miraculous Medal and recite the Memorare every day. He immediately was converted and begged for Baptism.

Our Lady of La Vang. Our Lady appeared in 1798 to Catholics who were in hiding in the jungle near La Vang, Vietnam. These Catholics were being persecuted by the Nguyen Dynasty and many were sick and starving. While they were praying the rosary in the evening, Our Lady appeared and told them to boil fern leaves for medicine. (La Vang means "the Fern.")

Church of Our Lady of La Vang, Santa Ana, CA.

Photos: The Shrine of Our Lady of Good Help,™ Diocese of Green Bay, WI.

Our Lady of Good Help. Our Lady appeared in Champion, Wisconsin, in 1859, to Adele Brise (above, and below with students), a Belgian Immigrant. At her third apparition, Our Lady revealed that she was the Queen of Heaven, and asked Adele to teach Catechism and pray for the conversion of poor sinners. This apparition is the first officially approved apparition of Mary in the United States.

Our Lady of La Salette. Images of Our Lady of La Salette as she appeared to Melanie Calvat and Maximin Giraud, near Grenoble, France, in 1846. She first appeared sitting on a rock with her hands covering her face. Standing, and telling the children to come nearer, she talked to them at great length, giving them many warnings about the punishments to come because of those who did not respect Our Lord's wishes. She then rose slowly into the sky and disappeared from sight.

Our Lady of Pellevoisin. *(right)* Our Lady appeared fifteen times in 1876, to Estelle Faguette in Pellevoisin, France. She revealed Estelle's past sins to her and obtained Estelle's cure from tuberculosis. Our Lady also revealed to Estelle the pattern for a scapular which she requested be made and promoted.

Our Lady of Knock. *(below)* Our Lady appeared to the villagers of Knock, in County Mayo, Ireland, on August 21, 1879. She appeared with St. Joseph to her right and St. John the Evangelist to her left. An altar with a lamb on top appeared to the left of St. John. The vision remained for two hours, and though it was raining the whole time, the ground where the vision was remained dry.

Joseph Kung, Cardinal Kung Foundation Orphanage.

Our Lady of China. Our Lady appeared to Chinese Christians who were being attacked during the Boxer Rebellion in China in 1900. St. Michael appeared along with her and chased the rebels away with a fiery sword. She appeared again in 1995 along with the Holy Family. This image of Our Lady of China is now kept by the underground Church in China due to attempts to confiscate it.

Our Lady of Fatima. *(left)* Our Lady appeared in 1917 to three shepherd children, Jacinta and Francisco Marto, and Lucia dos Santos. She told them to pray the Rosary every day and practice devotion to her Immaculate Heart.

Our Lady of Beauraing. *(below)* Our Lady appeared thirty-three times to five children in 1932 in the village of Beauraing in Belgium. She asked that the children be good and pray very much, and that people come there on pilgrimage.

Virgin of the Poor, Banneux. Our Lady appeared again in Belgium in 1933, in the village of Banneux, to a young girl named Mariette Beco. She called herself the Virgin of the Poor and directed Mariette to a stream which she said would heal the sick. Later a chapel was built, and many miracles were attributed to her intercession there.

Mary of the Rosary of San Nicolas. *(above)* Our Lady appeared to Gladys Quiroga de Motto in 1983 in Argentina. She requested that a chapel be built and a medal be struck in her honor.

Our Lady of Heede. *(left)* In 1937, Our Lady appeared to four young girls in Heede, Germany. She asked to be addressed as Queen of the Universe and Queen of the Poor Souls, and emphasized devotion to the Poor Souls.

OUR LADY OF BEAURAING
(THE VIRGIN WITH THE GOLDEN HEART)

Beauraing, Belgium
1932

THE BLESSED VIRGIN VISITS BEAURAING
THIRTY-THREE TIMES

THE little village of Beauraing is located about sixty miles southeast of Brussels, Belgium, and had about two thousand people at the time of the apparitions. Most of the people in the region made their living by farming, and some worked in nearby quarries and forests, while many had gardens which helped in supplementing their food supply. At one time, the people had been staunch Catholics, but by 1932, many had drifted away from the Church. Some were indifferent toward the Catholic Faith while others were hostile to it. Not helping the situation was the Labor Party which was Marxist and anti-Catholic, and which had carried the district in many elections. It was a time of unrest in the world as well, because the Communists were in power in Russia and were trying to extend their godless rule throughout the world. Benito Mussolini was master of Italy, and Adolf Hitler was soon to have complete power in Germany.

In this terrible world situation, the Blessed Virgin displayed her motherly concern by visiting Beauraing thirty-three times.

The visionaries were five children, four girls and one boy,

who belonged to two families. The children of the Voisin family were Gilberte, who was thirteen, Fernande, fifteen, and their younger brother, Albert, eleven. The two girls of the Degeimbre family were Andrée, fourteen, and Gilberte, nine.

It became a habit for four of the children to walk each evening to the Academy where Gilberte Voisin attended school until 6:30 p.m. When Gilberte was dismissed, the little group returned home.

Arriving at the convent school, which was operated by the Sisters of Christian Doctrine, they entered the gate and walked to their favorite place to wait, a garden that displayed a small Lourdes grotto. Beyond the garden was a street and above it a small bridge that crossed over it.

THE CHILDREN SEE THE VIRGIN

On November 29, 1932, while waiting for Gilberte, Albert was the first to notice a luminous lady walking on the bridge. He at once exclaimed, "It is the Virgin Mary walking atop the bridge." The figure then proceeded to move in mid-air toward the treetops within the garden. Albert's companions also saw the Lady, and when the nun opened the school door for Gilberte to leave, Gilberte also saw the Lady. Sister Valeria was alerted by the children, but she dismissed the story as simply child's play since she saw nothing.

The children excitedly informed their parents who were extremely skeptical but listened as the children described the beautiful Lady as wearing a long white gown with a silk veil that flowed down to where a small cloud covered her feet. They said that as the Lady drew near to them she seemed to emanate a bright light. Her hands were folded in prayer and she smiled at them, but said nothing.

THE SECOND VISION

The next evening, when Gilberte was leaving the school, all five children once again saw the beautiful Lady walking along the bridge. When they again reported it to their parents, their parents became furious and thought that someone was trying to scare them. The next evening, Mrs. Degeimbre took a stick with her to inspect the bushes for the prankster. While Mrs. Degimbre was thrashing the bushes, the children were heard to cry, "Oh, oh." This time the Lady was near the Lourdes grotto, her hands joined in prayer, her eyes raised to Heaven. She looked at the children, smiled and while rising from the ground, she disappeared.

THE THIRD VISION

For the next apparition, the Lady appeared under the arch of a hawthorn tree in the convent garden. It was there that she appeared for all the following visitations. During the early visions, the Lady did not carry a Rosary, but later there was always one suspended from her right arm.

For each of the visions, as soon as the children saw the lady they simultaneously dropped to their knees and recited the Hail Mary in high-pitched voices.

SEVERAL VISIONS OCCURRED TO THE CHILDREN

The children again described the vision as looking young, about eighteen or twenty; her eyes were a beautiful deep blue and rays of light formed around her head like a crown. She wore a long, white, heavily pleated gown without a belt. The children said that the dress reflected a kind of blue light and the Virgin's hands were pressed together as if in prayer, but she parted them as she vanished from sight.

On December 2, when the Lady again appeared, Albert made himself the spokesman of the group and asked: "Are you the Immaculate Virgin?" The lady smiled and nodded her head.

"What do you want?" Albert asked.

The Lady's first words were "Always be good." She appeared two more times that day and during the last time she asked: "Is it true you will always be good?"

"Yes," Andrée cried. "We will always be good." The Lady then disappeared.

Crowds began to form, but no one except the children saw the vision. When the Lady asked the children to return on the Feast of the Immaculate Conception, approximately fifteen thousand people assembled, expecting a great miracle. During this apparition, the children recited the Rosary while they waited for the Lady, who asked for a chapel to be built. During this apparition, a number of doctors made an attempt to distract the children during their ecstasy by pinching, slapping, by shining a flashlight in their eyes and even attempting to burn their fingers, but the children were unaffected.

Four days later, the Lady announced, "I am the Immaculate Virgin."

Fernande, on December 23, asked the Lady, "Why do you come?" The Lady answered: "That people might come here on pilgrimage." On December 29, the Blessed Virgin opened her arms in the usual gesture of farewell, and it was then that Fernande saw in the region of the Virgin's chest, a heart of gold surrounded by glittering rays. Our Lady then said, "Pray. Pray very much."

During the next vision, all the children saw the golden heart. In the following apparitions the Blessed Mother said, "I will convert sinners . . . I am the Mother of God, the Queen of Heaven. Pray always." Another time she gave a secret to each child and asked, "Do you love my Son? Do you love me? Then sacrifice yourself for me." During the last vision she showed her heart of gold, said, "Good-by," and disappeared. Some of the children wept in heart-wrenching disappointment.

THE VISIONS END

When the visions ended, the children visited the hawthorn tree each day to recite the Rosary. Their families never benefited financially from the visions, although they were frequently visited by the curious. In 1933, it was estimated that over two million pilgrims visited the hawthorn, which by then was protected by a bronze railing. Cures also bestowed legitimacy for unbelievers and many cures were investigated and regarded as miraculous. And, according to the Lady, many of the visitors were converted, including some Communists who at first meant to scoff and ridicule.

All of Belgium knew of the visions, and because of some criticism and opposition, the bishop almost immediately initiated an investigation in 1935. In 1936, Bishop Heylen consulted with Pope Pius XI who praised the heroic faithfulness of the children in going to the hawthorn every night for prayers. Many documents, studies and letters were circulated between the Holy Office, various cardinals and diocesan officials, so that by February 2, 1943, Bishop Charue accepted the validity of the visions of Our Lady of Beauraing and participated in official ceremonies celebrating the recognition. The Holy Father once again gave his personal approval of the apparitions by blessing the Sanctuary and the pilgrims in 1947. On July 2, 1949, Bishop Charue wrote to the clergy of his diocese:

> We are able in all serenity and prudence to affirm
> that the Queen of Heaven appeared to the children

of Beauraing during the winter of 1932–1933 especially to show us in her maternal Heart, the anxious
appeal for prayer and the promise of her powerful
mediation for the conversion of sinners.

The chapel that the Lady requested was built and consecrated on August 21, 1954. Many confessionals were added for
the converted sinners while the former Academy convent was
converted into a home for ill pilgrims.

None of the children were called to the religious life, instead,
they all married and raised their children in the good graces of
the Catholic Faith. The visionaries always shunned attention,
saying that they were merely instruments through whom Our
Lady gave her message to the world—one of the messages being
proof of her tender love for the world by the displaying of her
golden heart.

THE VIRGIN OF THE POOR
(OUR LADY OF BANNEUX)

Banneux, Belgium
1933

NEW VISIONS IN BELGIUM

ONLY twelve days after the apparition of Our Blessed Mother in Beauraing, Belgium, new visions were reported by a twelve-year-old girl at Banneux. It is understandable that many were suspicious since they supposed the local visionaries had appeared in imitation of those well-known apparitions of St. Bernadette. Some laughed and scoffed about the new apparitions in the small village, but one who took the matter very seriously was the young chaplain of Banneux, Abbé Louis Jamin, who was naturally concerned for the three hundred souls under his spiritual care.

THE FIRST APPARITION

Just as in Beauraing, the people of Banneux had drifted into indifference and boredom regarding the practice of their faith, but this changed when Mariette Beco of Banneux claimed to have visits from the Blessed Mother. Mariette was a strong, healthy girl who helped her mother around the house, and as the eldest, she acted as a babysitter and caregiver to her many siblings. That particular evening, January 15, 1933, at about seven o'clock, while the mother was busy in the kitchen and everyone else had gone to bed, Mariette sat up waiting for her brother Julien to return home; he had not been seen since noon. Looking out the window for him, Mariette noticed a glowing oval light in the small yard in front of the house. In the light stood a young, beautiful Lady who smiled graciously.

Mariette was at first awestruck by the wonder, but was practical in minutely examining the Lady, noting the gown, which was spotless and dazzlingly white and closed at the collar, and which fell in the simple dignity of broad pleats. The sash, an unforgettable sky blue, was loosely fashioned around the waist and ended in two streamers at the vision's left knee. Covering the Lady's head, shoulders and arms was a veil as white as her gown, but of a transparent material. The Lady leaned to the left with the hem of her dress slightly lifted, exposing her right foot which was crowned with a golden rose. On her right arm hung a rosary of diamond-like brilliancy, whose golden chain and cross were reflected in the light that enveloped her.

Mariette alerted her mother who went to the window, looked out and saw a mysterious light somewhat in the form of a woman. To this, she declared, "It is a witch," and closed the curtain. Mariette again looked out and seeing the Lady's reassuring smile, she began to pray with a rosary she had found by chance on a country road. After several prayers, the Lady did something that was unknown in her other visitations. She placed her left hand on her heart and lifted her right to the level of her head and beckoned with her index finger for Mariette to join her. When the young girl went to the door to leave, her mother barred the door. The Lady then disappeared.

The next morning her father, Julien Beco, who was a fallen-away Catholic, was skeptical and dismissed the incident as a reflection of light on the frozen snow. Reverend Jamin was informed, but he declared that it was an attempt to imitate the visions at Beauraing. He was surprised, however, when Mariette attended Holy Mass for the first time in months and additionally attended catechism class. After carefully questioning the girl, the good priest wondered if the vision was true. If her father returned to the sacraments, Father Jamin reasoned, then he would definitely believe in a miraculous happening.

THE SECOND VISION

The vision again appeared at about seven o'clock at night on January 18. Mariette had gone outside to await the appearance, and despite the cold, she knelt down and began the recitation of the Rosary. Her father was at her side trying with keen annoyance to persuade her to return to the warmth of the house. Then Mariette raised her arms. The Lady had returned. Gradually, the Lady approached from the direction of pine trees across the road, became larger and more luminous until she stood about five feet away from Mariette. All the while, the Blessed Mother stood on a gray cloud about a foot above the earth. The Lady seemed to join in the recitation, but did not touch the rosary which hung over her right arm. Then she beckoned for Mariette to follow her. With her father frantically calling her, Mariette simply answered, "She calls me."

The Lady floated on the cloud down the road and stopped three times, which caused Mariette to drop with a thud to her knees on the frozen earth. The father and two of his children followed at a distance and saw Mariette turn sharply right and fall to her knees on the side of a ditch before a previously unknown spring. The Lady directed Mariette to place her hands in the water. As Mariette's hands splashed the water, she repeated the words of the Lady, "This stream is reserved for me. Au revoir." The lady then disappeared. Mariette awoke from a trancelike state after the Lady's thirty-five-minute visit.

An hour later, Father Jamin was informed of the happening, and in the company of a Benedictine priest, they stopped at the Becos' house. On the way, Fr. Jamin mentioned to his companion that he would believe in the vision if, "for example, Mariette's father were converted."

THE THIRD VISION

The next evening, January 19, Mariette again started to pray as she knelt in the snow. In a moment, she excitedly announced, "Oh, she is here." To her question, "Who are you, lovely Lady?" the Lady answered, "I am the Virgin of the Poor." Once again Mariette followed the Lady to the spring and knelt down beside it as she posed her second question, "Beautiful Lady, you said yesterday, 'This spring is reserved for me.' Why for me?" The Lady was amused and declared: "This spring is reserved for all nations—to relieve the sick." The Lady then said, "I shall pray for you. Au revoir." She then disappeared. The vision had lasted only seven minutes.

THE FOURTH VISION

The next evening, January 20, with about thirty people waiting outside to witness the vision, Mariette joined them on the gravel walk in front of the house. When the Lady appeared, Mariette asked, "What do you wish, my beautiful Lady?" The Virgin of the Poor answered, "I would like a small chapel." Before the Lady vanished, she unfolded her hands from their prayerful position, imposed them on Mariette, and then with her right hand, blessed Mariette with the Sign of the Cross. In response, Mariette fainted.

THE FIFTH VISION

The Virgin did not appear again until February 11, but during the interval, Mariette and her family were harshly criticized. In school, Mariette endured the taunts of her classmates while her father, who had converted, was ridiculed by the local Socialists. But on February 11, after reciting the Rosary as she had every evening, Mariette fell into a trance and began walking to the spring while reciting the Hail Marys. When she reached the water source, she knelt down before the beautiful Lady. She placed her hand in the water and blessed herself while listening silently to the Lady. Afterward she responded with, "Thank you, thank you."

THE SIXTH VISION

The next few days brought bad weather and there were no visions, but on February 15, while again praying the Rosary, the Virgin of the Poor appeared. Mariette asked her, "Blessed Virgin, the chaplain told me to ask you for a sign." Mariette listened carefully as she was given a heavenly secret. She then dissolved in tears. To the crowd's many questions, she answered, "The Virgin said, 'Believe in me, I will believe in you. Pray much. Au revoir.'"

THE SEVENTH VISION

The Lady did not appear again until February 20 when she and Mariette went down the road to the stream. This time the Lady appeared unsmiling and spoke: "My dear child, pray much. Au revoir."

THE FINAL APPARITION

The final apparition, the eighth, occurred on March 2. After a heavy downpour, the Lady appeared during the recitation of the Rosary. Mariette listened carefully as the Lady revealed: "I am the Mother of the Saviour, Mother of God. Pray much." Then after listening to another of the Lady's messages, Mariette kept repeating, "Yes, yes." Once again the Blessed Mother stretched out her hand and blessed Mariette. This final apparition lasted five minutes.

The little chapel requested by the beautiful Lady was built and inaugurated during the year of the apparitions, 1933, with the first reported miraculous cures taking place that year. In fact, between 1933 and 1938, twenty-five physical cures met the rigid tests of medical records and were declared to be of miraculous origin.

The investigation by the Episcopal Commission began its deliberations in 1935, and submitted its finding to Rome in 1937. The bishop, Msgr. Louis Joseph Kerkhofs of Liège, approved the visitations of the Virgin of the Poor, which received its final approval on August 22, 1949. The statue of Our Lady was solemnly crowned in 1956.

In a letter written by Pope John Paul II to the bishop of Liège dated July 31, 1999, on the occasion of the fiftieth anniversary of the recognition of the apparitions, the pope recounted:

> I myself, during my Apostolic Visit to Belgium in May 1985, I had the joy of celebrating in this shrine which has an important outreach. I gladly join in the prayer of the pilgrims who go there to seek comfort and strength from Our Lady of Banneux, invoked by the name of Our Lady of the Poor, Health of the Sick.

Every year at least a half million people visit the shrines, one of which was built near the Beco house and the other over the spot where Our Lady appeared at the spring. The water of this spring was capped and its source directed to multiple outlets in the wall that extends along both sides of the spring.

Mariette decided to remain a private person, married and led a quiet family life.

OUR LADY OF HEEDE
(QUEEN OF THE UNIVERSE)
(QUEEN OF THE POOR SOULS)

Heede, Germany
1937

THE FIRST APPARITION

TWENTY years after the dramatic apparitions at Fatima, Our Lady appeared to four young girls with almost the same message. The event first took place on November 1, 1937. The four girls were: Anna Schulte, Greta and Maia Gauseforth and Susanna Bruns who were on their way to church when they passed the church's cemetery and saw the Blessed Virgin who appeared to them with the Divine Child in her arms. This news coming from playful and usually giddy girls was accepted with the usual enjoyment, skepticism and laughter. But when all four girls changed their manner of living to a more serious demeanor with long and fervent prayer, the people began to wonder. Even so, the pastor and most of the villagers refused to believe in the apparitions for some time until they noticed how the devout girls waited nervously and expectantly for the next visit of the Mother of God.

News of the apparitions spread quickly to surrounding towns and villages with crowds converging at the apparition site. Many however were fearful of visiting Heede, since at the time Hitler ruled Germany and forbade participation in this "superstitious nonsense." Hoping to put a stop to the activities at Heede, the Gestapo forcefully took the children to a mental hospital and strictly forbade the pilgrimages. Soon after, the children were released, and, disregarding the orders of the Gestapo, they resumed their visits to the place of the apparitions.

THE BLESSED VIRGIN CONTINUED TO APPEAR

The Heavenly Queen was not subject to the Hitler regime and continued her appearances in secret locations. The Lady emphasized devotion to the Poor Souls in Purgatory and warned the children of the impending chastisement of God's justice. After being asked how she would like to be addressed, the vision replied, "As Queen of the Universe and Queen of the Poor Souls." She also indicated her love for the Litany of Loreto.

It was only after many cures were reported and verified that the parish priests and other clergymen supported the visionaries. Like almost all her apparitions elsewhere, this vision consisted of only a few words being spoken—these being similar to the message of Fatima in which the Lady asked for prayer, repentance and conversion.

THE BLESSED MOTHER APPEARS FOR THE LAST TIME

The apparitions of the Blessed Mother came to an end on November 3, 1940, when she appeared for the last time in the church cemetery as she had done during the first apparition. The Lady at this time said to the children: "Be good and resigned to the will of God. Pray often, especially the Rosary. Now, farewell, my children, until we meet in Heaven."

OUR LORD APPEARS TO GRETA GANSFORTH

Following the last appearance of Our Lady, Our Lord then began His visitations in 1945, when He appeared to Greta Gansforth and gave a lengthy warning to the world.

> Men did not listen to My Most Holy Mother when she appeared to them at Fatima and admonished them to do penance. Now I Myself am coming at the last hour to warn and admonish mankind! The times are very serious! Men should at last do penance, turn away from their sins and pray, pray much in order that the wrath of God may be mitigated. Particularly the Holy Rosary should be prayed very often. The Rosary is very powerful with God. Worldly pleasures and amusements should be restricted.
>
> Men do not listen to My voice, they harden their hearts, they resist My grace, they do not wish to have anything to do with My mercy, My love, My merits; mankind is worse than before the deluge. Mankind is suffocating in sin. Hatred and greed rule their hearts. This is the work of the devil. They live in great darkness. Through the wounds that bled, mercy will again gain victory over justice. My faithful souls should not be asleep now like the disciples on Mt. Olivet. They should pray without ceasing and gain all they can for themselves and for others.
>
> Tremendous things are in preparation; it will be terrible as never before since the foundation of the world. All those who in these grave times have suffered so much are martyrs and form the seed for the renovation of the Church. They were privileged to participate in My captivity, in My scourging, in My crown of thorns and My Way of the Cross

The Blessed Virgin Mary and all the choirs of angels will be active during these events. Hell believes that it is sure of the harvest, but I will snatch it away from them. I will come with My peace. Many curse me now, but these sufferings will come over mankind that they may be saved through it . . . Many expiate all they can for those who curse Me now.

With a few faithful I will build up My kingdom. As a flash of lightning this Kingdom will come . . . much faster than mankind will realize. I will give them a special light. For some this light will be a blessing; for others darkness. The light will come like the Star that showed the way to the wise men. Mankind will experience My love and My power. . . . My beloved, the hour comes closer. Pray without ceasing!

When the apparitions commenced, the bishop appointed a new parish priest to examine, with a committee, the details of the apparitions. In the end, the Bishop of Osnabruck declared the apparitions to be "undeniable proofs of the seriousness and authenticity of these manifestations . . . In the apparitions and messages of Heede we find nothing contrary to the Faith; indeed, their similarity to the approved apparitions of Fatima, Lourdes and La Salette give good indications of their authenticity."

Our Lady of Sorrows

La Codosera, Chandavila, Spain
1945

THE FIRST VISION

*J*T WAS three in the afternoon, May 27, 1945, when ten-
year-old Marcelina Barroso Exposito, accompanied by
her cousin, Augustina, was walking to the village on an
errand for her mother. The girls walked through the area known
as Chandavila when they noticed something strange in the distance. They were about to ignore it, but then a strange force
somehow propelled them to a chestnut tree. There, a little above
the ground, was a vision of Our Lady of Sorrows. She was easily
identified by the black robe and mantle she wore, the stars that
sparkled around her and the stars that embellished her gown.
Her hands were joined and her beautiful face bore every mark of
deep pain and overwhelming sadness.

Marcelina alone saw the Lady, and when the vision disappeared she ran with her cousin to the village where her message
was greeted with great excitement.

THE SECOND VISION

Days later, on the morning of June 4, Marcelina returned
to the place of the apparition and beheld the Virgin once again.

This time the Lady spoke, telling her to return in the afternoon when she would ask the girl to perform a sacrifice in the presence of all who attended.

Accompanied this time by a thousand people, both Spanish and Portuguese, Marcelina walked to the apparition site in an ecstatic condition that drew wide attention. After arriving in sight of the chestnut tree, she stopped and beheld the vision in the distance. The Lady invited the girl to crawl on her knees to her, a distance of about one hundred feet, and reassured her, "Fear not. Nothing will harm you. I will be putting before you a reed mat and herbs so that you will not be hurt."

Upon seeing her daughter in an ecstatic state and crawling on her knees over rocks and rough ground, Marcelina's mother fainted. The child, however, remained for about ten minutes kneeling by the tree. Then, in addition to the vision of the Virgin, the child saw a beautiful church and on the altar appeared the Virgin Mary who invited the child to dip her fingers in holy water and bless herself. When the child drew near to the Virgin, she was asked if Marcelina would like to join her in Heaven. The child answered enthusiastically, "Yes, Ma'am, now." The Blessed Mother smiled and kissed the child on the forehead. While doing this, the mantle of the Mother of God softly touched Marcelina's face. The Virgin then requested that a chapel be built at the place of the apparition.

When the vision disappeared, Marcelina was no longer ecstatic and began talking with her friends. They, on the other hand, paid particular attention to her knees and found no scratches or injuries after seeing her crawl over rough ground. The pastor of Codosera, Father Juan Antonio Galan y Galan, also checked for injuries, but found none.

While accompanied each time by more and more people, Marcelina had other encounters with the Blessed Mother. She eventually enrolled in a Catholic school in Villafranca de Los Barros near Badajoz. Later, in Seville, on August 2, 1975, she became a religious in the Congregation of the Sisters of the Cross and took the name Sister Mary of Mercy of the Cross. She was a member for many years in this Order, which was dedicated to the care of the sick, orphans, the poor and elderly. After a time she joined a cloistered convent in Ciudad Real.

ANOTHER VISIONARY APPEARS

The history of the apparition at Codosera now includes another visionary. While Marcelina was still experiencing the visions of Our Lady of Sorrows, Afra Blanco Brigade, then seventeen years old, went to Codosera with her friends on May 30, 1945. Like the other pilgrims, Afra wanted to see Marcelina, to witness the event and to take part in the prayers that were offered there. Upon her arrival, she thought she saw something dark in the clouds. The next day, she again went to the place of the apparition and once again saw the dark object. This time it drew nearer until it was clearly recognized as Our Lady of Sorrows. The vision proved to be overwhelming for Afra who fell into a deep faint.

A few days later, Afra's grandmother died. While Afra was dressed in mourning, her friends approached her and insisted that she join them for another visit to the place of the visions, which she did. While kneeling next to Marcelina, the apparition revealed herself to both girls. This time the Lady told Afra a secret, predicted great suffering and then asked her to kiss Marcelina. She asked for the recitation of the Rosary and the construction of a chapel.

Days later, Afra and Marcelina went to Villar del Rey and stayed there from July 21 until July 24, giving thanks to the Virgin Mother for all the favors received.

STIGMATA APPEAR ON AFRA BLANCO BRIGADE

While making the Way of the Cross there, Afra became ecstatic at the eleventh station and saw the sufferings of Our Lord and his Crucifixion. Suddenly she felt a sharp pain on the palms of both hands and discovered that an incision in the center of each was dripping blood and causing excruciating pain. Eventually, the stigmata were present on both feet and then were seen to penetrate deeper into the hands. The pain continued and the blood flowed mainly on Fridays in commemoration of Our Lord's Crucifixion. Afra underwent numerous medical examinations, but treatments to heal the wounds were unsuccessful. It was noted that the stigmata were accompanied by a sweet fragrance.

Afra worked for many years in a hospital in Madrid until her death on August 23, 2008, at the age of eighty, after a long and painful illness.

After completing her schooling, Marcelina Barroso Exposito joined the religious Order known as the Congregacion de Hermanitas de la Cruz. Known as Sr. Maria of the Mercy of the Cross, she worked until her death caring for the sick, orphans, and the poor.

A beautiful church, which enveloped the chestnut tree of the apparition, was eventually built. The permission for the construction of this church, as well as approval for the Expression of Faith, was given by the Bishop of Badajoz.

MEDIATRIX OF ALL GRACES

Marienfried, Germany
1946

JUST as at Fatima when an angel appeared to the visionaries and introduced prayers in preparation for the apparitions of the Queen of Heaven, so, too, here at Marienfried, Germany, an angel appeared to the amazement of twenty-two-year-old Barbara Reuss.

The event took place in Marienfried, near Paffenhofen, on the twenty-fifth day of April, May and June, 1946.

AN ANGEL AND THE BLESSED MOTHER APPEAR TO BARBARA REUSS

In the first apparition in April, an angel appeared calling himself "the Angel of the Great Mediatrix of Graces." He instructed Barbara to kneel while he addressed a prayer to the Blessed Virgin Mary. This was his prayer: "Act as the Mother of Grace; act as the thrice miraculous Mother; the thrice admirable Mother of Grace, Thou Great Mediatrix of Graces!" As the angel recited this prayer, the Blessed Virgin appeared in a brilliant light. She was "unspeakably beautiful, brilliant, a blinding vision of the most pure light and radiance . . . Above her head were brilliant rays forming a three-tiered crown." As the Immaculate Queen raised her hand in blessing, she became as transparent as crystal, and so bright that Barbara was unable to look at her.

THE SECOND AND THIRD APPARITIONS

Many people accompanied Barbara for the second apparition, and for the third visit, the pastor, Fr. Humf, and his sister were present. The messages almost repeat those of Our Lady at Fatima in which she requests the recitation of the Rosary, devotion to the Holy Trinity and consecration to her Immaculate Heart. The Virgin also warned of future events. Her messages were lengthy, but here is a compilation of some of her wishes:

> I am the powerful Mediatrix of Graces. As the world can find mercy only through the sacrifice of the Son with the Father, so can you find favor with the Son through my intercession. Christ is unknown because I am not known. It is true that the world was consecrated to my Immaculate Heart, but this consecration has become a fearful responsibility for many men. I demand that the world live the consecration.
>
> I am the sign of the Living God. I place my Sign on the foreheads of my children (those who consecrate themselves to my Immaculate Heart). Lucifer will persecute the sign, but my sign will conquer. . . . Substitute my Immaculate Heart in place of your sinful hearts. . . . Fulfill my request so that Christ may reign as the King of Peace.
>
> The world will have to drain the cup of wrath to the dregs because of the countless sins through which His Heart is offended. The devil of the infernal regions will rage more violently than ever and will cause frightful destruction because he knows that his time is short, and because he sees that

already many have gathered around my sign. Over these he has no spiritual power, although he will kill the bodies of many; but through these sacrifices my power to lead the remnant host to victory will increase . . .

Pray, make sacrifices for sinners. Pray the Rosary. Pray not for external things—weightier things are at stake in these times. Expect no signs and wonders. I shall be active as the powerful Mediatrix in secret.

The devil will be possessed of such power that those who are not firmly established in me will be deceived. . . . You should establish everything in confidence to my Immaculate Heart. The devil has power over all people who do not trust in my heart . . .

In secret I shall work marvels in souls until the required number of victim souls will be filled. Upon you it depends to shorten the days of darkness. Bishops and priests should consecrate themselves to me. . . . Pray always. Pray the Rosary. Keep the Saturdays which have been dedicated to me. . . . If you consecrate yourselves without reserve, I shall take care of all the rest. . . . The Father pronounces a dreadful woe upon all who refuse to obey His Will.

A PRAYER GIVEN AT THE THIRD APPARITION

After the Blessed Mother stopped speaking, she was suddenly surrounded by an immense number of angels wearing long white garments. Kneeling on the earth they bowed deeply and recited a homage to the Holy Trinity. On its completion, the angel, who had been present during the first apparition, asked Barbara to repeat the prayer.

Suspecting that a message, or a special prayer, would be given during this third apparition, Father Humf was prepared to write down what was said. Although he did not know what was taking place during the vision, he wrote the following prayer as Barbara repeated it and as requested by the angel. In a soft, rhythmic voice, Barbara began:

> Praise to You, eternal Ruler, living God, always Being, fearful and righteous Judge, always kind and merciful Father. Your radiant Daughter will always worship, praise, honor and obey you.

The Bishop of Augsburg, after reviewing all aspects of the apparitions, rendered a decision in March 2000, in which he declared that the faithful are free to conduct pilgrimages and services at the Marian Shrine.

OUR LADY OF PRAYER

L'Ile Bouchard, France
1947

WHEN the Soviet Union was intent on expanding their influence in France, they were involved in acts of sabotage throughout the country. Trains were being derailed, food shortages were becoming more severe than they were during the World War that had recently ended, and there were general strikes that threatened the economy that was already on the verge of collapse. General chaos had the French government so worried they recalled over one hundred thousand reservists to help defend France in case of civil war and the country's total collapse.

In the midst of all this confusion, our Blessed Lady came down to help her children by appearing in the little church of Saint Giles in the village of L'Ile Bouchard that was located in the northwestern part of France, in the Archdiocese of Tours. It was the only church in the village which also had only one school that was attended by fifty pupils.

The children had attended school on December 8, 1947, which was to be a very special day. Not only was it the feast of the Immaculate Conception, but it would also be remembered as being the first apparition of Our Lady of Prayer.

During the day the nuns who taught at the school encouraged the children to pray for France which was in terrible danger. Three little girls, Jacqueline Aubry, aged twelve, her sister

Jeanette, aged seven, and their cousin Nicole Robin, aged ten, had eaten their lunch at home and were returning to school when Jacqueline Aubry suggested they stop on their way to make a visit to the chapel of the Blessed Mother in the church. On arriving at the altar of the Virgin they began to recite a decade of the rosary and were not quite halfway through when they looked up and saw a beautiful Lady with her hands joined in prayer; a white rosary hanging from her right arm. To the left of the Lady was an angel, holding a lily while his eyes were fixed in contemplation of the Lady.

While the beautiful Lady smiled at them, Jacqueline whispered that other people should see the vision as well and ran outside to notify others. She immediately came upon their school friends Laura Croizon, aged eight and her sister Sergine, aged thirteen. Returning to the church Laura immediately saw the apparition while the oldest, Sergine, could not and had to be told what was happening.

The children described the Lady as being very beautiful. She was wearing a brilliantly white dress with gold trim at the neck and wrists. There was a blue sash around her waist while her head was covered with a veil. Its white color, they said, was different than the dress. On close inspection the girls noticed that it was decorated along the edges with motifs known as "Touraine" which was popular in their region of France. The girls noticed that the lady's hands were joined in prayer and that she radiated a strong golden light. They also noted that her eyes were blue and they estimated her as being sixteen or seventeen years of age. Unusual to this apparition was the Lady's long blond hair that fell down on either side almost to her knees. The Lady stood on a stone block that was decorated with a garland of five pink roses. On the rock, written in gold were the words, "O Mary, conceived without sin, pray for us who have recourse to thee," words made familiar during the apparitions of our Lady at Lourdes.

The angel was described as kneeling on his right knee. He

wore a robe which was a soft rose color. He, too, had blue eyes and long blonde curly hair. In his left hand he held a lily stalk while his right hand was placed over his heart. His white wings were trimmed in gold while his feathers moved slightly in a breeze that the children could not feel. During the whole of the vision he seemed to be in profound contemplation of Our Lady.

The area of the church during the apparition was lit by a light with colors that the girls had never seen before. Eventually the apparition disappeared into what they could only describe as a cloud of silvery dust.

After the apparition faded the children returned to school and excitedly told Sister Marie de L'Enfant Jesus who immediately believed them while the parish priest, Fr. Clovis Segelle did not, although he questioned the girls extensively.

After school ended, the children returned to the church and were delighted to see the Lady beckoning them. The Lady seemed extremely sad as she slowly uttered: "Tell the little children to pray for France, for her need is great."

Jacqueline wondered about the Lady's identity and asked if she were the "*Maman du Ciel*" ("Heavenly Mother"). The Lady replied, "But of course I am your *Maman du Ciel*."

On inquiring about the angel, he turned toward the girls and said: "I am the angel Gabriel."

The next day, December 9, at one o'clock, the four girls assembled in the church as the Lady had requested the previous day. While praying a decade of the rosary the Lady appeared in a shining golden sphere. Her hair, which had intrigued the children before, was now hidden by her veil while across her breast was written in gold letters the word "Magnificat." The words on the rock now read, "I am the Immaculate Conception."

The apparition lifted high the golden crucifix of her rosary and asked the girls to kiss it. Jacqueline and Nicole stood up to do this, while to the surprise of all present, the two shorter girls, unable to reach the crucifix, were lifted up by Jacqueline as though they were weightless. Once again the vision asked the girls to "Pray for France, which is in great danger." The Lady also asked that a grotto be built and that her image and that of the angel should be placed in it.

Fr. Segelle, who had already questioned the girls a number of times, informed the archbishop of what had occurred. That same day, to the surprise of the region, the Communists decided to abandon plans of a general strike.

The next day, Wednesday, December 10, approximately one hundred and fifty people were awaiting the appearance of the Virgin. During this apparition, Jacqueline's mother called out to her daughter telling her to request a miracle so that all would believe. To this Mary replied, "I have not come here to perform miracles, but to tell you to pray for France." Then addressing Jacqueline, who wore thick glasses and had to wipe her eyes often because of chronic conjunctivitis, the Lady told her, "Tomorrow you will see clearly and will no longer have need of glasses." The Virgin then disappeared into a golden ball of light.

When Jacqueline awoke the next morning she was able to open her eyes without difficulty and discovered that she had normal vision. Her overjoyed father then rushed to tell Fr. Segelle about the miracle to which news the priest exclaimed, "So it is true that she has descended among us!"

The next day, December 11 at one o'clock the church was full of people. The vision asked the children if they had prayed for sinners to which they replied that they had. Then Mary led them through ten Hail Mary's, but she only said the first part of the prayer, the words with which the angel Gabriel had greeted her at the Annunciation.

Three hundred people were present on December 12 when Mary appeared wearing a crown composed of twelve sparkling rays each about a foot long. These were interspersed with smaller ones of various colors. After listening to the singing of the Hail Mary, the Virgin led the children in ten Hail Mary's of the Rosary, again pronouncing only the words of the angel Gabriel. The word "Magnificat" was again visible in letters across her chest.

A crowd of about five hundred attended the vision the next day. During the vision the Blessed Virgin appeared without the crown and to Jacqueline's request for a miracle that all would believe, the reply was, "Later." The child was then told that the last apparition would take place the following day.

The church of St. Giles that day was crowded with people who began praying the rosary. The Blessed Mother and the angel appeared and remained for over a half hour. The Lady requested that the Magnificat be sung which Fr. Segelle sang reverently with the people. After this the Virgin asked for more prayers for sinners and in response to the request for a miracle, Mary responded with a smile: "Before I go I will send a bright ray of sunlight." After blessing the people the Lady vanished, but a mysterious bright ray of sunshine streamed through a window and settled on the very place of the apparition. It grew in strength and size so that all had to shield their eyes. As for the children, they were surrounded by sparkles of various colors.

The ray of light was later determined to be inexplicable in natural terms since it would normally have been interrupted by some of the pillars of the church. Subsequent tests proved that it was physically impossible for a normal ray of sunlight to have entered that part of the church at that time of the year because of the position of the sun. It was therefore determined to have been a miraculous occurrence.

Fr. Segelle examined the girls separately as he did after all the apparitions and found them to be truthful and to have agreed on all the details of the vision. Archbishop Honore, who was the archbishop of Tours at the time, after carefully studying the facts of the apparitions, authorized the construction of the grotto requested by the Lady and permitted pilgrimages to the church. He also sanctioned the veneration of Our Lady under the title of "Our Lady of Prayer."

Forty-one years later, in November 1988, after several investigations were performed by noted ecclesiastics, the grotto was built and statues of Our Lady and the angel, in the attitude of the vision, were placed in the church of St. Giles. Monsieur Piquot, the Secretary General of the Interior Ministry, having heard of the events in L'Ile Bouchard, immediately went to meet the girls, and in front of the whole community declared, "France was saved by the prayers of these four children and by the people here who prayed at the feet of the Virgin Mary." Subsequent theological investigations followed and all proved favorable including the most recent one headed by French theologian Father Vernet in 1992. Following this was Bishop Andre Vingt-Trois of Tours, who, in a Decree dated December 8, 2001, declared: "Having carefully studied the events, and taken council with appropriate persons, I authorize these pilgrimages, and all manner of public worship."

OUR LADY OF ZEITOUN
(OUR LADY OF LIGHT)

Zeitoun, Cairo, Egypt
1968–1971

AFTER the birth of Jesus, when King Herod heard that a new king of the Jews had been born, "he became greatly disturbed, and with him all Jerusalem" (Matt. 2:2–3). In order to rid himself of a threat to his position, "He ordered the massacre of all boys two years old and under in Bethlehem and its environs" (Matt. 2:16). Before this took place, an angel appeared in a dream to Joseph with the command: "Get up, take the child and His Mother, and flee to Egypt. Stay there until I tell you otherwise. Herod is searching for the child to destroy Him" (Matt. 2:13–14). According to scripture, the Holy Family left that night for Egypt.

During their journey through the country, they paused at different locations along the way. Each stop, sanctified by their presence, later became a place of prayer, often marked by a small chapel. Some of these buildings grew through the years into handsome structures dedicated to the Holy Family, others developed into monasteries, and some into beautiful churches such as St. Mary's Coptic Church in Zeitoun-Cairo, a church dedicated long ago to the Holy Mother. It was here that the Blessed Mother made several nightly appearances that were seen by millions.

THE FIRST APPARITION

It all began an hour and a half after sunset, Tuesday, April 2, 1968. As workmen were leaving a nearby garage, they heard a disturbance in the street. Joining the anxious crowd, they saw a young lady dressed in white walking on the dome of the church. Thinking she was about to throw herself down, they cried, "Be careful, take care. You will fall." Others cried aloud, "It is the Virgin Mary." Because the workmen were Muslim, they were thoroughly perplexed. One of these men, Muslim Farouk Mohammed Atwa, had been undergoing operations for a case of gangrene, and the following day the hospital that had examined and treated him declared that he was completely healed.

Traffic along the street was stopped as crowds of people gathered to see the vision. The Lady appeared in a luminous body. She walked about on the roof and was seen to often bow or kneel before the cross. The priest of the church, Father Costantin, was alerted and he, too, saw the figure. Another observer was Abdul Nasser, president of Egypt who was a self-proclaimed Marxist.

Accompanied by beautiful lights and immense clouds of incense, the Lady sometimes appeared clearly, sometimes opaquely. She was seen to walk about, to bow or kneel before a cross, to smile, bow and wave an olive branch. Some saw the vision clearly while some people saw nothing at all. Many viewers were transfixed, while many prayed the Rosary and sang Christian hymns.

At times the Lady was accompanied by small white figures resembling doves that would fly in the figure of the cross. They would also fly about her and suddenly vanish from sight. None of the birds, however, were seen to flap their wings.

The apparitions were photographed, televised, witnessed by millions, written about in the international secular and religious press and seen by people of all nationalities and religions.

Soon His Holiness, Pope Kyrillos VI, organized a committee

of priests and bishops to investigate the events. As a result, on May 4, 1968, the Coptic Orthodox Church officially confirmed the apparitions. Also confirming the appearance of the Blessed Mother were Dr. Henry Ayrout, of the local Catholic college of the Jesuit Order and Rev. Dr. Ibrahim Said, the head of all Protestant Evangelical Ministries in Egypt. Catholic nuns of the Sacre-Coeur Order witnessed the apparitions and sent a detailed report to the Vatican. An envoy from the Vatican soon arrived, saw the apparition on Sunday, April 28, 1968, and also sent his report to His Holiness Pope Paul VI in Rome. The report in its entirety is given here:

*The Official Statement from the Papal Residence in Cairo on the Apparition of Saint Mary in the Zeitoun Coptic Orthodox Church in Cairo, Egypt.**

> Since the evening of Tuesday, April 2, 1968, the apparitions of the Holy Virgin Saint Mary, Mother of Light, have continued on the Coptic Orthodox Church named after Her in Zeitoun, Cairo.
>
> The apparitions occurred on many different nights and were continuing in different forms. The Holy Virgin Saint Mary appeared sometimes in full form and sometimes in a bust, surrounded with a halo of shining light. She was seen at times on the openings of the domes on the roof of the church, and at other times outside the domes, moving and walking on the roof of the church and over the domes. When she knelt in reverence in front of the cross, the cross shone with a bright light. Waving her blessed hands and nodding her holy head, she

---

* http://zeitun-eg.org/zeitoun1.htm, access date 5/9/2012.

blessed the people who gathered to observe the miracle. She appeared sometimes in the form of a body with a very bright cloud, and sometimes as a figure of light preceded with heavenly bodies shaped like doves moving at high speeds. The apparitions continued for long periods, up to two hours and fifteen minutes as in the dawn of Tuesday, April 30, 1968 when she appeared continuously from 2:45 a.m. till 5:00 a.m.

Thousands of people from different denominations and religions, Egyptians and foreign visitors, clergy and scientists, from different classes and professions, all observed the apparitions. The description of each apparition as of the time, location and configuration was identically witnessed by all people, which makes this apparition unique and sublime.

Two important aspects accompanied these apparitions: The first is an incredible revival of the faith in God, the other world and the saints, leading to repentance and conversion of many who strayed away from the faith. The second are the numerous miracles of healing which were verified by many physicians to be miraculous in nature.

The Papal Residence has thoroughly investigated the apparitions and gathered information by way of committees of clergy who have also witnessed the apparitions themselves and recorded everything in reports presented to His Holiness Pope Kyrillos VI.

By issuing this statement the Papal Residence declares, with full faith and great joy and humility of a thankful heart, that the Holy Virgin Mary, Mother of Light, appeared in clear forms on many different nights, for periods of variable length, lasting on occasion more than two continuous hours . . . It is historically proven that the location of this church in Tumanbay Street, in Zeitoun quarter, on the way to El-Mayarya, Cairo, *is on the path taken by the Holy Family when visiting Egypt.*

May God make this miracle a symbol of peace for the world, and a blessing for our nation as it has been prophesied: "Blessed be Egypt My people."

The report was dated Saturday, May 4, 1968.

So widespread did the reports of the apparition become by virtue of television, newspapers and the media reports, that a massive project was inaugurated to restore and renovate the church both inside and out, which has already taken place.

Roman Catholic Cardinal Stephanos investigated the happenings thoroughly, including the miraculous cures and the many conversions, and submitted his report to Pope Paul VI in May 1968. The Pope was quick to approve the events as a visitation of the Mother of God.

OUR LADY OF AKITA

Akita-Shi, Japan
1973

ISTER Agnes Katsuko Sasagawa was forty-two years old when she joined a small group of devout women known as the Institute of the Handmaids of the Holy Eucharist who lived quiet, hidden lives of prayer in Yuzawadai on the outskirts of Akita. At the time, Sister Agnes, a convert from Buddhism, was totally deaf.

THE FIRST VISION

Exactly one month after her acceptance, an extraordinary event took place when something like fog gathered around the altar in the little convent church. Then a multitude of angels surrounded the altar in adoration before the Sacred Host. When this first apparition took place, Bishop Ito was staying at the convent to conduct a week of devotions. Sister Agnes confided the occurrence to the bishop as well as the convent's spiritual director, Rev. Teiji Yasuda, both of whom witnessed events that would take place later. Sister's Guardian Angel frequently visited her, but the most extraordinary event took place on the evening of June 28, 1973, when Sr. Agnes discovered a cross-shaped wound on the palm of her left hand that caused excruciating pain. A small opening appeared in the center from which blood began to flow.

The next morning, July 6, 1973, Sister's Guardian Angel suggested that they pray together in the chapel before the image of the Blessed Mother. This statue had been carved from the hard wood of the Judea tree in 1965, by M. Saburo Wakasa, a Buddhist sculptor renowned in the area. The statue of Our Lady is about three feet tall. She stands before a large cross with her arms at her side and the palms of her hands facing forward. Beneath her feet is a globe representing the world.

When sister approached the statue, "I suddenly felt that the wooden statue came to life and was about to speak to me. . . . She was bathed in a brilliant light . . . and at the same moment a voice of indescribable beauty struck my totally deaf ears." The Lady promised, "Your deafness will be healed." The vision recited a community prayer with Sr. Agnes, but at the words, "Jesus present in the Eucharist," the vision instructed, "From now on you will add TRULY." The Lady then suggested, "Pray very much for the pope, bishops and priests . . ."

The following morning, when the sisters assembled for the recitation of the Office, they discovered blood on the right hand of the statue and a wound which perfectly resembled that on the hand of Sr. Agnes. It was noticed that while the blood ran the length of the statue's hand, which was open and pointing downward, the drops never fell from it.

The wound on the hand of Sr. Agnes appeared on Thursday, June 28, and disappeared, as predicted by the Guardian Angel, on Friday, July 27, without leaving a trace.

A message from Our Lady came on August 3, 1973,

> Many men in this world afflict the Lord. . . . In order that the world might know His anger, the Heavenly Father is preparing to inflict a great chastisement on all mankind. . . . I have prevented the coming of calamities by offering Him the sufferings of His Son on the Cross, His Precious Blood and beloved souls who console Him forming a

cohort of victim souls. Prayer, penance and coura-
geous sacrifices can soften the Father's anger . . .
know that you must be fastened to the Cross with
three nails. These three nails are poverty, chastity and obedience. Of the three, obedience is the
foundation.

Although the wound on the hand of Sr. Agnes disappeared
on July 27, the wound on the hand of the statue remained until
September 29 when it left in a brilliant light. The wound had
remained for three months.

While the whole community was at prayer on September
29, they saw a resplendent light coming from the statue. Almost
immediately, the entire body of the statue became covered with
a moisture resembling perspiration. Sister's Guardian Angel
informed her, "Mary is even sadder than when she shed blood.
Dry the perspiration."

The moisture was collected on clumps of cotton, some of
which were sent to the University of Akita for analysis. The finding was that the liquid was of human origin, and, moreover, had
a pleasant, heavenly fragrance.

The third and final message of Our Lady came on October
13, 1973, the anniversary of the great miracle of Fatima. While
reciting the Rosary, Sr. Agnes again heard the heavenly voice
warning the world.

As I told you, if men do not repent and better themselves, the Father will inflict a terrible punishment
on all humanity. It will be a punishment greater
than the deluge, such as one will never have seen
before. Fire will fall from the sky and will wipe out a
great part of humanity, the good as well as the bad,
sparing neither priest nor faithful. The survivors
will find themselves so desolate that they will envy
the dead. The only arms which will remain for you
will be the Rosary and the sign left by my Son. Each

day recite the Rosary. With the Rosary, pray for the pope, the bishops and the priests.

The work of the devil will infiltrate even into the Church in such a way that one will see cardinals opposing cardinals, bishops against other bishops. The priests who venerate me will be scorned and opposed by their confreres . . . Churches and altars sacked; the Church will be full of those who accept compromises and the demon will press many priests and consecrated souls to leave the service of the Lord.

The demon will be especially implacable against souls consecrated to God. The thought of the loss of so many souls is the cause of my sadness. If sins increase in number and gravity, there will be no longer pardons for them . . . Pray very much the prayer of the Rosary. I alone am able still to save you from the calamities which approach. Those who place their confidence in me will be saved.

Toward the end of May 1974, another phenomenon occurred when the face, hands and feet of the statue became a dark, reddish-brown tint, while the garments and hair remained the same. On January 4, 1975, another phenomenon took place when the statue began to weep and did so three times that day. Witnessing the event were the nuns and Bishop Ito.

Father Yasuda, the chaplain of the convent wrote in his book, *The Tears and Message of Mary*, that the statue

> . . . had completely dried out during the years since it was made and little cracks had begun to appear. It is already miraculous if water would flow from such material, but it is still more prodigious that a liquid slightly salty, of the nature of true human tears, should have flowed precisely from the eyes.

When the sculptor of the statue examined his work in 1979, he replied:

> The statue of Mary was my first work connected
> with Christianity. Of my various statues, it is only
> with the statue of Mary that mysterious events
> occurred. . . . I sculptured the whole statue of Mary,
> globe, and the Cross from the same piece of wood,
> so there are no joints. . . . The wood from which I
> carved the statue of Mary was very dry and rather
> hard.

When questioned as to whether he regarded the events as a miracle, he replied, "*Fushigidesu.*" ("It is a mystery.")

The weeping of the statue occurred one hundred and one times at irregular intervals from January 4, 1975, until September 15, 1981. Most of the weepings were witnessed by people of all ranks and ages, both non-Christian and some prominent Buddhists, including the mayor of the city. Some of the events were recorded by television cameras and shown throughout the country.

As predicted by Our Lady, Sister's deafness was cured on May 30, 1982.

In a pastoral letter dated April 22, 1984, Bishop John Shojiro Ito wrote,

> I authorize throughout the entire diocese of which I
> am charged, the veneration of the Holy Mother of
> Akita . . . I have known Sr. Agnes for ten years. She
> is a woman sound in spirit, frank and without prob-
> lems; she has always impressed me as a balanced
> person. Consequently the messages she says that she
> has received did not appear to me to be in any way
> the result of imagination or hallucination.

Four years later, on June 20, 1988, during Bishop Ito's visit to Rome, the Sacred Congregation for the Doctrine of the Faith approved the contents of his pastoral letter. In August 1990, Cardinal Ratzinger, the present Pope Benedict XVI, was quoted as saying that "there are no objections to the conclusion of the pastoral letter." The Cardinal also invited Bishop Ito to continue to inform him about the pilgrimages and conversions.

Reconciler of People and Nations
(Our Lady of Betania)

Betania, Venezuela
1976–1990

THE FIRST MYSTICAL EXPERIENCE OF
MARIA ESPERANZA

MARIA Esperanza, a married woman and mother of seven, had thirty-one visions of the Blessed Mother at this place that the Church has officially declared is "sacred ground." Numerous phenomena have also been reported there and witnessed by many.

The visionary was born November 22, 1928. Her first mystical experience took place early when Maria, who was only five years old, had a vision of St. Theresa of Lisieux who gave her a rose. The Blessed Mother also demonstrated her special interest in Maria when the child was seven years old and near death from pneumonia. The Mother of God appeared to Maria and recommended the appropriate medication which hastened her recovery.

From her earliest years, Maria felt called to the religious life and entered the Order of the Franciscan nuns in Merida. Unfortunately, her dream was not to be realized because the Mother Superior determined that Maria did not have a vocation. St. Theresa of Lisieux consoled Maria and revealed that her vocation lay in the married state and as a mother. Subsequently, on December 8, 1956, the Feast of the Immaculate Conception, while on a visit to Rome, Maria married Geo Bianchini in Saint Peter's Basilica. This marriage would produce seven children, a boy and six girls who were also called to the married state and, in time, had children of their own.

Some years later, in 1974, Maria and her husband purchased a farm a few miles from Caracas which the Blessed Mother predicted would become a center of "constant prayer and pilgrimage" for "all the nations of the world."

The first apparition on the farm took place on March 25, 1976. Maria described the appearance of the Blessed Mother in this manner,

> When she revealed herself, she went to the top of the tree, and I saw she was beautiful, with her hair brown, dark brown, her eyes that were light brown and she had very fine, very pretty eyebrows, a tiny mouth, a nose very straight and her complexion was so beautiful, it was skin that seemed like silk. It was bronzed. It was beautiful. Very young. Her hair was down to here, to her shoulders.

As the Blessed Virgin had predicted years earlier, the farm soon became a place of pilgrimage with over one hundred people seeing the Virgin at the grotto in 1984. An unusual aspect of the place is that Maria does not have to be present for phenomena to take place. Sometimes when Maria is not present, the Virgin reveals herself, sometimes in mysterious manifestations in clouds or in a type of haze.

The Virgin appeared thirty-one times to Maria asking for prayers for the Reconciliation of Peoples and Nations. Of these visions, twenty-four took place after 1984.

During these apparitions and subsequent visits by pilgrims, more than five hundred miracles and cures have been reported while over two thousand testimonials were given that claim various celestial phenomena.

Maria herself,was favored with the stigmata. She is known to have been surrounded by a sweet aroma, to have had the gifts of healing, levitation, bilocation and the capability of predicting future events, and to have been blessed not only with visitations of the Blessed Mother, but also with apparitions of her beloved Son.

Approval of the events at Betania was declared on November 21, 1987, by Bishop Pio Bello Ricardo who declared,

> After having studied repeatedly the apparitions of the Most Holy Virgin in Betania, and having begged the Lord earnestly for spiritual discernment, I declare that in my judgment the said apparitions are authentic and have a supernatural character. I therefore approve, officially, that the site where the apparitions have occurred be considered as sacred."

Likewise Bishop Freddy J. Fuenmayor, Bishop of Los Teques decreed

> I declare the sacred place where the image of Our Lady has been venerated under the title of Mary Reconciler of All People and Nations, a Marian diocesan sanctuary of Our Lady."

THE LAST VISION

The last vision of the Blessed Mother took place on January 5, 1990.

But a wonderful manifestation of another sort took place the following year on December 8, 1991, when, on the Feast of the Immaculate Conception, during Holy Mass offered by Father Otty Ossa Aristizabal, the consecrated Host began to bleed. Tests later made in Caracas proved that the blood was of human origin.

After a life of numerous phenomena and heavenly visitations, Maria died of a Parkinson-like ailment in a New Jersey hospital, on August 7, 2004, surrounded by her family.

Our Lady of Cuapa

Cuapa, Nicaragua
1980

THE FIRST VISION

ℬERNARDO Martinez was the sacristan of the church in Cuapa and had arrived to ring the bell to alert the parishioners for the recitation of the Rosary when he saw a brilliant light coming from the shrine of Our Lady. His only thought then was the expense of the unnecessary lighting of the church. Although he cannot remember the exact date, he does remember that on April 15, 1980, he saw the shrine bright once again and upon inspection saw the statue of the Virgin illuminated. Thinking that the boys playing outside had somehow damaged the church to let in the light, he realized on inspection that the light was definitely coming from the statue.

> This was a great mystery for me, with the light that came from her one could walk without tripping. And it was nighttime, almost eight o'clock at night . . . I then understood that it was a strange thing.

When news of the happening reached the parish priest he asked for a description of the vision and also wanted to know what were the usual prayers that Bernardo recited. The sacristan replied, "I told him I recite the Rosary and three Hail Mary's to the Holy Virgin ever since I was little. I was also taught to say when I had any tribulations: "Don't leave me, my Mother." The priest then advised him to keep the vision secret and not to report any future events to the parishioners.

This first apparition was a silent one, but on May 8, 1980, things were different. Bernardo tells that one night he felt sad because of financial, employment and spiritual problems. He had been ridiculed because his work at the church was so menial: sweeping, dusting and washing altar linens. He spent a restless night, but in the morning he thought he would go fishing and enjoy the peace and tranquillity of the isolation.

THE SECOND VISION

He was walking home with his collection of fish when suddenly there was a flash of lightning followed by another. To his amazement, a beautiful Lady was standing above a group of rocks but was actually supported by a brilliant cloud. Bernardo describes the vision in this way:

> I was wondering if it was the same statue as in the chapel, but I saw that she blinked . . . that she was beautiful. On the cloud were the feet of a very beautiful lady. Her feet were bare. The dress was long and white. She had a brilliant cord around the waist. Long sleeves. Covering her was a veil of a cream color with gold embroidery along the edge. Her hands were held together over her heart. It looked like the statue of the Virgin of Fatima.
>
> I saw that she had human skin and that her eyes moved and blinked . . . she extended her arms like the Miraculous Medal that I had never seen before, but which later was shown to me. She extended her arms and from her hands came rays of light stronger

than the sun . . . the rays that came from her hands touched my heart. I asked her "What is your name," and she said, "My name is Mary . . . I come from heaven. I am the Mother of Jesus." She requested that the Rosary be said in a family group, including children and it was to be prayed at a set hour when there were no problems with the work in the home.

She told me that the Lord does not like prayers we make in a rush or mechanically . . . She recommended praying the Rosary with the reading of biblical citations (the Scriptural Rosary). She later recommended the propagation of the devotion to the shoulder wounds of Christ.

The Lady also wanted the renewal of the five first Saturdays and warned, "If people do not change there will be grave dangers and they will hasten the arrival of the Third World War."

When the cloud began to rise, the vision raised her arms to Heaven as in the statue of the Assumption and gradually vanished from sight.

Hoping to avoid another vision that might bring him ridicule if he told of it, he decided to avoid the river where she had first appeared and instead walked through a pasture in search of a missing cow. While he was walking, the Lady again appeared, preceded by lightning flashes. She promised him help in relating the vision. This filled his soul with peace and allowed him to tell what had happened with no fear of ridicule.

During the night of June 8, the Lady favored him with a detailed dream in which he was shown Dominican and Franciscan monks and groups of people praying the Rosary in procession. He was also granted a nighttime vision of an angel who foretold several events which eventually occurred. The Blessed Mother again appeared in September, but this time as a child. During the course of the apparition, when Bernardo asked her whether the people of his parish should build a new church they had been planning, she said, "The Lord does not necessarily want a material Church, He wants living temples which are yourselves."

The last apparition took place on October 13, during which the people experienced a strange phenomenon. After reciting the Rosary and while singing the hymn *My Queen of Heaven*,

> a luminous circle formed on the ground. The light came from above and marked the area . . . I looked up and saw that a circle had also formed in the sky. Everyone present, without exception saw it. During this apparition the Blessed Virgin's garments changed to a grey color, her face became sad and she cried. She said through tears: "It saddens me to see the hardness of those persons' hearts. But you will have to pray for them so they will change."

No doubt inspired by the Blessed Mother's apparitions, it is reported that Bernardo Martinez became a priest and served the people of Nicaragua with dedication.

The apparitions have found favor with a number of bishops including Archbishop Pio Bello Ricardo in 1987, and in 1982, Bishop Bosco M. Vivas Robelo and the Vicar General of the Archdiocese of Manague as well as Bishop Pablo Antonio Vega, the Prelate Bishop of the diocese where the apparitions took place. In 1987, Archbishop Pio Bello Ricardo wrote "I approve the site for pilgrimages as a place for prayer, meditation and worship . . ." and on May 26, 2009, Bishop Freddy J. Fuenmayor of Los Teques wrote:

> In the exercise of my faculties as Bishop of Finca Betania, and the tenor of Canon 1230 of the Canonical Code . . . I declare the place a Marian diocesan sanctuary of Mary Reconciler of all Peoples and Nations.

Our Lady of Sorrows

Kibeho, Rwanda
1981–1983

T HE small country of Rwanda is seen by some as the heart of the continent and one of its most beautiful areas, where plantations of tea and coffee abound. Visitors have named it the Land of Eternal Spring. But at the time of the apparitions, the country was in a state of unrest. Statues of the Blessed Mother were mutilated or destroyed and priests, influenced by the propaganda of false theologians, were lax in their duties and beliefs. Only two devout priests maintained the true principles of the Faith and the teaching of sound doctrine, which influenced most of the people of Rwanda to the fervent practice of the Catholic Faith.

To correct the morals of the region and to plead for the restoration of religion, the Blessed Virgin appeared to Alphonsine Mumreke who was seventeen years old. Alphonsine was a student in a school that was run by three nuns and various lay teachers. There she was known to have been very pious and to have shown a great love of the Mother of God.

THE FIRST APPARITION

The first apparition took place in the school on Saturday, November 28, 1981. Alphonsine was in the dining room serving her classmates that day when she was startled by a sweet voice that called her. Since she did not see anyone around her who spoke her name, Alphonsine went into the hallway and saw a most beautiful Lady who announced that she was the "Mother of the World," and had come in answer to her prayers.

Alphonsine described the Lady in this way,

> The Virgin was not white as she is usually seen in holy pictures. I could not determine the color of her skin, but she was of incomparable beauty. She was barefoot and had a seamless white dress, and also a white veil on her head. Her hands were clasped together on her breast, and her fingers pointed to the sky. Later I was told by my classmates that I had been speaking in several languages: English, French, Kinyarwanda and others. When the Virgin was about to leave I said three Hail Marys and the prayer, Come Holy Spirit. She then rose to heaven like Jesus.

Alphonsine remained kneeling in a state of ecstasy for more than fifteen minutes while the nuns and staff members attempted to rouse her. When Alphonsine finally began to stir and spoke of the apparition, the faculty thought she was sick.

THE SECOND APPARITION

Another apparition took place the next day, November 29, and was repeated almost every Saturday in December. During these visitations, Alphonsine's classmates attempted to test her by pricking her with needles or trying to burn her with matches. They also waged a subtle persecution by heaping upon her all types of verbal abuse, saying among other things that she had lost her mind.

Eventually, because of various phenomena, which included sparkling lights and the appearance of a star, both faculty and students came to believe, and even gave Alphonsine their rosaries for the Blessed Virgin to bless.

While the daytime visions took place in the dining room, the evening visits took place in the dormitory, in the room of Alphonsine. Eventually, as news spread about the miraculous events, the apparitions began to take place in the school yard where thousands gathered.

To the surprise of all, Our Lady began appearing to another student, Anathalie Mukamazimpaka and then to Marie-Claire Mukangango who had been one of the most vocal opponents of the apparitions. Marie-Claire declared, as a result of an apparition, that "One must meditate on the Passion of Jesus, and on the deep sorrows of His Mother. One must recite the Rosary every day, and also the Rosary of the Seven Sorrows of Mary, to obtain the favor of repentance."

Alphonsine experienced a mystical journey on March 20, 1982. After informing the nuns that she might appear to be dead while this was taking place, she would nevertheless be very much alive. During the eighteen hours in which this ecstasy took place, priests, nurses, religious and medical assistants for the Red Cross, all saw that Alphonsine appeared to be in a deep sleep, was rigid, and had clasped hands that could not be separated. Alphonsine later revealed that the Blessed Mother had shown her Heaven, Purgatory and Hell.

During these visitations, the Blessed Virgin gave many messages for the world. Calling herself the Mother of the World, she announced that the purpose of her visitations was to communicate a message of conversion through a life of prayer and confession, a life renewed by the Word of God and by works of charity and justice. The Blessed Mother told Marie-Clare that she was addressing herself to the whole world which is in revolt against God and is "on the edge of catastrophe."

During other apparitions, Anathalie described the visions in this way:

In July 1982, and the following months, August
15, 1982, the feast of the Assumption, and again
on September 4, and in January 1983, Our Lady
showed us many things about the coming war.
Often she talked in general that the world is bad,
that people do not have love, contrary to what God
shed His blood for; Our Lady insists as well on love.
Our Lady talked about and showed us some visions
of reality where people killed each other, blood running, fire burning on the hill, mass graves, skulls,
beheaded bodies, skulls put apart.

Anathalie continued: "Our Lady appeared to remind us
what we have forgotten. In her messages she insisted on prayer
and on conversion, on penance and humility."

The Blessed Mother's last visit to the visionaries was on
August 19, 1982, during which she revealed the consequences of
those who would ignore what she recommended. Like the vision
of Anathalie, the other visionaries also saw "a river of blood,
people who were killing each other, abandoned corpses, trees all
in flames, bodies without heads."

About a decade later, in the spring of 1994, a vicious civil
war erupted in Rwanda in which an estimated 500,000 to
800,000 people were killed; many beheaded by machetes and
dumped into the Kagea River. Many were killed by friends or
neighbors in the genocide that lasted one hundred days.

The Blessed Mother had also warned that sexual promiscu-
ity would lead to disaster—this before the world experienced the
AIDS epidemic. By 1994, Africa had 70 percent of the world's
cases. It is estimated that several million Africans fell victim to
the disease.

It was during the war that the visionary, Marie-Clare, was
killed. It is said that she had married Elie Ntabadahiga in 1987,
and had moved to Kigali to be with him. According to eyewitnesses, Elie was taken prisoner by the militants, and when

Marie-Claire begged for her husband's release, she was murdered. As for the other visionaries, Alphonsine is now a cloistered nun living in the Saint Claire convent of Abidjan, Ivory Coast. Her religious name is Alphonsine of the Glorious Cross. Anathalie still lives in the Kibeho parish where she is dedicated to preparing the church and the altar for Holy Mass.

It was after the civil war that the Catholic Church made a definitive ruling regarding the apparitions of Alphonsine Murmureka, Anathalie Mukamazimpaka and Marie-Claire Mukangango. Although four others are said to have witnessed the apparitions, approval for the visions of the original three was granted by Bishop Jean-Baptiste Gahamanyi who was in charge of the Diocese of Butare at the time of the visitations. On July 2, 2001, the Vatican released the declaration of Bishop Augustin Misago of Gikongoro who expressed approval of the visions after examinations were conducted by both medical and theological examiners. The original summary of their studies consisted of a twenty-three-page document.

Bishop Augustin Misago declared, "There are more reasons to believe this than to deny it," and that "the events corresponded satisfactorily to all the criteria established by the Church in the matter of private apparitions and revelations."

Pope John Paul II, during his visit to Rwanda in 1990, exhorted everyone to turn to the Virgin Mary as a sure guide to peace and salvation.

Mary of the Rosary of San Nicolas

Buenos Aires, Argentina
1983–1990

GLADYS Quiroga de Motto was a housewife, a mother of two daughters and a grandmother who had no knowledge of theology or the Bible, and had only a fourth-grade education. She kept to herself and was never comfortable with the attention she received as a result of her visions. No doubt because of her simplicity and humility, the Blessed Mother visited her numerous times during a period of seven years, requesting conversions, consecrations and the praying of the Holy Rosary.

THE FIRST VISION

A strange phenomenon introduced the appearance of the Blessed Virgin when Gladys saw a gentle glow illuminating a rosary that hung on the wall of her bedroom; in the same place where the Blessed Virgin would later appear. This was witnessed by her neighbors, some of whom, sometime later, also saw their rosaries with a similar glow.

The first apparition of the Blessed Mother took place on September 25, 1983, and again three days later. But it was on October 7, the Feast of Our Lady of the Holy Rosary, while Gladys was praying the Rosary, that she spoke to the apparition for the first time. Gladys reports that, "I saw her (the Blessed

Mother) and I asked her what she wanted of me." The apparition remained silent and then faded away, but was replaced by the vision of a chapel. Gladys remembered, "I understood that she wanted to be among us."

Gladys discussed her experience with the parish priest who suggested that she sprinkle the vision with holy water. Later he advised her to write down all her experiences, including all the words spoken by the vision.

Then on October 13, the Blessed Mother again appeared and spoke to Gladys for the first time. Because of the advice given her by the priest, Gladys sprinkled the apparition with holy water. When the sprinkling did not disturb the vision, Gladys inspected the vision carefully and described the Blessed Virgin in this way:

The Virgin's figure glowed with light. She wore a blue gown and a veil and held the Baby Jesus in her arms along with a large Rosary.

Another time she gives more of a description:

Today I wish to say how I see the Most Holy Virgin Mary. Her beauty is not easy to describe, but she is beautiful, and in her the humility, the force, the purity and the love . . . because all the love of the world I believe that it does not cover the love that she feels for her children. When she orders, I feel the force that she has. When she gives advice, I feel her maternal love. And when she says to me that she suffers for those that have moved away from the Lord, she transmits her sadness to me. All this leaves in me this wonderful Mother to whom I have consecrated my life. I do this so that my dear brothers can know somehow how our Heavenly Mother is.

An extraordinary event took place on the evening of November 24, when a shaft of light pierced the darkness and indicated the place where the chapel was to be built: a wasteland called Campito on the banks of the nearby Parana River. Not only did Gladys see the piercing light, but also many villagers as well. Three days later, during an apparition, the Virgin Mary referred to Exodus 25:8 which reads, "They shall make a sanctuary for me, that I may dwell in their midst." This refers to the Israelites building an Ark of the Covenant as a dwelling for God, having obtained instructions from Him as to the design. In the church requested by Our Lady, it would be her Ark of the Covenant, her dwelling place in the midst of her people.

Later that month, Gladys met with the newly installed bishop of San Nicolas, Domingo Salvador Castagna, who listened to her with great interest. Later, while in Rome on other business, he arranged for an interview with Pope John Paul II. As a result of this meeting in April 1985, a Commission of Inquiry was named.

A MEDAL IS STRUCK

In May of the same year, the Blessed Virgin requested that a medal be made.

> You must strike a medal with my image and the words 'Mary of the Rosary of San Nicolas.' On the reverse side the Holy Trinity with seven stars. These represent the seven graces which my Son, Jesus Christ, will grant to all who wear it on their chest.

The medal was struck according to the Virgin's instructions and gained enormous popularity.

The foundation for the new sanctuary was laid on September 25, 1986, and it was on October 13, 1987, the anniversary of Our Lady of Fatima, that the construction of the sanctuary began in earnest.

When Pope John Paul II was on a pilgrimage to Argentina, Bishop Castagna, on April 11, 1987, met him in the city of Rosario and once again consulted with His Holiness about the continuing apparitions and promised to conduct a full study, which was concluded in February 1990.

When the church was nearing completion, a statue of the Blessed Virgin was needed for the altar dedicated to her. It was then that the people remembered that a statue that had been blessed in Rome by Pope Leo XIII, the "Pope of the Rosary," had been stored in the belfry of the cathedral because of damage and deterioration. It was taken down, repaired and placed on the altar reserved for it in the new church. When Gladys saw the statue for the first time, she exclaimed that it closely resembled the Blessed Virgin as she appeared in her apparitions.

Even before the sanctuary was completed, pilgrims came in procession from distant places. They continue to come, especially on the twenty-fifth of each month, which commemorates the anniversary of the first vision. Their confidence in Our Lady was rewarded with a number of spiritual and physical healings. The many answers to these prayers prompted Bishop Castagna, on July 25, 1990, to declare: "Undoubtedly this event of grace will continue to grow; it has proved its authenticity by its spiritual fruits."

One month later, the bishop consecrated the sanctuary to the Immaculate Heart of Mary and was pleased to issue an *Imprimatur* for the Spanish edition of the Messages of Our Lady to Gladys de Motta.

A replica of the statue of Mary of the Rosary of San Nicolas holding her Son was blessed by Pope John Paul II at the Vatican in the year 2000, but it was Pope Benedict XVI who blessed the crosses that adorn the crowns worn by the Mother and the Child Jesus.

Our Lady of Shoubra

Cairo, Egypt
1986–1991

THE Blessed Virgin Mary favored the overcrowded quarter of Shoubra and the little church of Saint Demiana the Martyr by appearing atop the church on numerous nights, starting on Tuesday, March 25, 1986. On that date, the Lady appeared between the two towers of the church and was seen by the people living in the houses nearby. They were alerted to the vision when their homes became illuminated by the light that shone around the vision. While looking for the source of the light, they discovered to their surprise that the Lady was on the roof of the church. They saw her in full body, surrounded by a halo of light. When the people of the area heard about the vision, and it appeared again the next night, the narrow street in front of the church became crowded with the curious who promptly recognized the vision as the Mother of God. In awe and reverence, they began singing hymns while many began the recitation of the Holy Rosary.

Newspaper and television reporters were soon alerted, so that the phenomenon was broadcast throughout Egypt and the world. The Coptic Pope Shenouda III lost little time in issuing a papal order announcing the formation of a special committee which numbered six members, four of whom were bishops. The committee examined the accounts of eyewitnesses, and on Thursday, April 10, 1986, at midnight they went to the church to closely examine all that was taking place. To their satisfaction and wonder, they saw the Holy Virgin in a clear form surrounded by a halo of light between dawn and 5:00 a.m.

The committee met again and, after examining witnesses, learned that the apparition of the Virgin appears in different forms. Incense is noted and white doves fly about. There was a very luminous and radiating, unnatural light that appeared inside the church tower that also shines to the outside. The light continued even though the whole quarter should have been dark when the electric power was turned off to perform a test. The Coptic Pope Shenouda III in his statement following the committee's results, stated:

> Let us thank the Lord for this blessing on the people of Egypt and for the repetition of these spiritual phenomena. . . . We are contented to take from these apparitions their blessings, the satisfaction of the saints and the positive action of these matters in our hearts.

The report of the committee was sent to the Holy Synod that was assembled on June 21, 1986. It reported that the apparitions were not limited to night hours, but also occurred during the day; that they were not limited to the church towers but also occurred inside the church on the eastern side of the altar. The apparitions were not limited to the Blessed Mother because others also appeared, including the Child Jesus and the martyr Saint Demiana who held a green palm, just as she appears in one of the church's icons. The apparitions, they noted, were repeated over a long period of time and that they still occurred on June 20, 1986, as witnessed by a delegation. They were informed that not only a luminous glow surrounded the Virgin, but also, at times, even flames of fire.

Published in the Watani newspaper of April 20, an article told of the Virgin surrounded by a transparent light, that the

Virgin wore a halo of light and that she looked at the crowds and often extended her arms toward them in blessing. The report tells that white doves were often seen, sometimes flying in formation with their wings extended, but not flapping them. It was revealed that the Blessed Mother was seen wearing white and sometimes blue or red colors. The Lady, it was recorded, also appeared inside the church in a normal size sometimes surrounded by luminous colors, and that a measure of light that appeared by the altar circulated three times around the church over the heads of the people.

To the delight and spiritual enrichment of the people, the apparitions of Our Lady of Shoubra continued until the year 1991.

A statement from the Coptic Orthodox Papal Delegation of April 1986, states, "We are contented to take from these apparitions their blessings, the satisfaction of the saints and the positive action of these matters in our hearts."

OUR LADY OF ASSIUT

Assiut, Egypt
2000–2001

THE third apparition of Our Lady in Egypt, which is very similar to the others, is said to have taken place where the Holy Family sought refuge from the threats of King Herod. Assiut has a 40 percent Coptic population and hundreds of mosques. It was also known as one of the main centers of Islamic fundamentalism. Yet, the Blessed Virgin deigned to appear numerous times on the roof of St. Mark's Church, in full size, between the main towers of the church. She moved about and was often seen with lights emanating from her outstretched hands. To the delight of many, the appearances were often accompanied by the scent of incense and with oversized, brilliant white doves flying about, sometimes in formation.

DAZZLING LIGHTS SURROUND THE VIRGIN

The appearance of dazzling blue-green lights that flashed over the church was a source of wonderment to all. The skeptics, however, believed them to be laser beams or other unusual lighting. The confusion about the lights was so widespread that the electrical current in the neighborhood was turned off as a test. Still the Heavenly Lady was visible and the Heavenly lights continued. About these mysterious lights, Father Labis from the nearby Copt Dronka Monastery declared, "If you look for the source of the lights, you can't find it. This is light from heaven."

It did not take long for many church officials and city officials to give statements regarding the apparitions. Father Mina Hanna, the secretary of the Assiut Council of Churches reported that the sightings were "a blessing for Assiut." His Holiness Shenouda III stated that the apparitions "are a message of comfort from Heaven and one of confirmation of the faith of Copts, that heaven is aware of their struggle and is pleased by their perseverance."

THE APPARITIONS ARE VIEWED BY MANY

The apparitions stirred the secular world as well, with the BBC News reporting details of the happenings, as well as ABC News and countless newspapers around the world. Even television stations gave either live coverage or taped segments revealing the lights. Cameras of the witnesses were also busy, and many of their photos were shown on various web sites.

It has been reported that thousands of Egyptians have flocked to Assiut, which is located more than three hundred miles south of Cairo. By the end of the visions, it was estimated that more than two million persons were witnesses to the apparitions.

Like the other apparitions in Egypt, Assiut has also been associated with a great spiritual revival, the conversion of sinners and countless miracles of healing.

Our Lady of El-Warraq

Warraq al-Hadar, Giza, Egypt
2009

APPARITION ON THE COPTIC CHURCH

*T*HE little church that was named in honor of the Virgin Mary and the Archangel Michael was relatively unknown outside the country, but on the night of December 11, events took place that would be known throughout the world.

On that night, a huge crowd gathered in front of the church while phone calls poured into the rectory of the parish priest, Father Dawoud. As Father wrote, "The phone calls were of people who said they had just seen an apparition of the Virgin Mary on the right dome of the church." Father explained that Muslim neighbors were among the callers, including Haj, a neighbor and a dear friend who told me, "What are you doing here, Father? I have just seen Our Lady Mary with my own eyes. Go and see for yourself."

At first we thought that a little child was playing with a flash light, but then the light intensified and moved from the tree in front of the church entrance up to the right dome and an embodiment of the Virgin Mary could be easily recognized. She stayed there for a while.

It is of especial benefit to hear the statement of a credible witness, especially when the witness is a bishop. In this case, it was the Coptic Orthodox Bishop Theodosios of Giza who issued a statement,

> On Friday, December 11, at 1 a.m., the Holy Virgin appeared at her full height in luminous robes above the middle dome of the church. Her dress was pure white and she wore a royal blue belt. She had a crown on her head, above which appeared the cross. The crosses on top of the church's domes and towers glowed brightly with light. The Holy Virgin moved between the domes and onto the top of the church gate between the twin towers. The local residents all saw her. The apparition lasted from 1 a.m. until 4 a.m. on Friday and was recorded by cameras and cell phones. Some 3,000 people from the neighborhood, those from surrounding areas, and passersby gathered in the street in front of the church to see the apparition.

The bishop continues:

> I stayed up all night and saw doves appear suddenly in the sky. They flew in circles in front of the church before they vanished into thin air. They were floating rather than hovering with their wings.

The bishop noted that doves do not usually fly at night. The bishop also mentioned that a star appeared suddenly and traveled across the sky before disappearing. Bishop Theodosios continued, "The huge crowd gathered around the church did not cease singing hymns and praises for the Holy Virgin." The Copts accepted the apparitions as a sign of love and approval since they coincided with the beginning of the Coptic month of Kiahk, better known as "Mary's month" which is dedicated to praising the Virgin's conception of Christ and the ending of the Coptic Church's Christmas celebration.

As for the Episcopal approval of the visions, His Holiness

Shenouda III and Anba Dumadius, Archbishop of Giza, issued a statement which described the apparition and ended with a prayer. "This is a great blessing for the church and for all the people of Egypt. May her blessing and intercession benefit us all."

Apparitions Organized by Country

BIBLIOGRAPHY

Auletta, Gennaro. *The Blessed Bartolo Longo.* The Shrine of Pompeii. Pompeii, Italy. 1987.

Amatora, OSF, Sister Mary. *The Queen's Heart of Gold, The Complete Story of Our Lady of Beauraing.* Exposition Press. New York. 1957.

Ashton, Joan, *Mother of All Nations.* Harper & Row publishers. San Francisco. 1989.

Barbedette, Oblat, Raconte, Joseph. *Pontmain, Recit d'un Voyant. La Journée du 17 Janvier 1871.* The Sanctuaire de Pontmain. Pontmain, France.

Bibliotheca Sanctorum. Citta Nuova Editrice. Volume XI. Roma. 1968.

Brown, Raphael. *Saints Who Saw Mary.* TAN Books and Publishers, Inc. Rockford, Illinois. 1955.

Caggiano, Pietro. *The Shrine of Our Lady of the Rosary of Pompeii.* Santuario Beata Vergine. Pompeii, Italy. 1997.

Carillo, Argentina. Pasquale Mocerino. Loreta Somma. *Pompeii, Illustrated Guide to the Shrine of the Rosary.* Editions of the Shrine of Pompeii. Pompeii, Italy. 2009.

Carmelite Tertiary. *Carmelite Devotions.* The Bruce Publishing Company, Milwaukee. 1956.

Catholic Encyclopedia. Robert Appleton Company. Encyclopedia Press, Inc. New York. 1913.

Chourry, Jean-Baptiste, Pierre Jouandet, Rene Point, *Jean-Louis Peydessus.* Nôtre-Dame de Garaison. Monleon-Magnoac, France. 1981.

Connell, Janice T. *Meetings With Mary, Visions of the Blessed Mother.* Virgin Publishing. London, England. 1998.

Couessin, Pierre de. *Apparitions de Marie en Bretagne a Querrien.* Salvator. Paris, France. 2007.

Coyne, William D. *Our Lady of Knock.* Catholic Book Publishing Company. New York. 1948.

Cruz, Joan Carroll. *Miraculous Images of Our Lady.* TAN Books and Publishers, Inc. Rockford, Illinois. 1992.

Delaney, John J., Editor. *A Woman Clothed With the Sun.* Image Books. Garden City, New York.1959.

Franciscan Friars of the Immaculate. *You Will Make This Known To All My People.* New Bedford, Massachusetts. 1998.

Gallotti, G. *Santuario Basilica Madonna Della Misericordia.* Santuario Basilica. Savona, Italy.

Garcia, OFM, Fray Antonio Corredor. *Que Ocurrio en La Codosera?* Cofradia de Ntra. Sra. De los Dolores de Chandavilla. La Codosera, España. 1997.

Histoire du Sanctuaire. Shrine of Nôtre-Dame de Garaison. Monleon-Magnoac, France. 1999.

Ilibagiza, Immaculée, with Steve Erwin. *Our Lady of Kibeho, Mary Speaks to the World from the Heart of Africa.* Hay House, Inc. New York. 2008.

Johnston, Francis W. *The Wonder of Guadalupe.* TAN Books and Publishers, Inc. Rockford, Illinois. 1981.

Johnston, Francis W. *The Voice of the Saints.* TAN Books and Publishers, Inc. Rockford, Illinois. 1986.

Kennedy, John S. *Light on the Mountain, The Story of La Salette.* McMullen Books. New York. 1953.

Larrouy, Père A. *Histoire de Notre-Dame de Garaison.* Papers. Shrine of Notre-Dame de Garaison. Monleon-Magnoac, France.

Laurentin, René. *The Apparition at Pontmain.* Sanctuaire de Pontmain. Pontmain, Belgium. 2001.

Makulski, Father Eugeniusz, MIC. *Our Lady of Lichen.* Wydawnictwo ZET. Wroclaw, Poland. 2001.

Message of Marienfried, According to Our Lady's Apparitions in 1946. AMI International Press. 1970. Pamphlet.

Mocerino, Pasquale. *The Blessed Bartolo Longo.* Editions of the Shrine of Pompeii. Pompeii, Italy. 2006.

Mullen, Peter. *Shrines of Our Lady.* St. Martin's Press. New York. 1998.

Nôtre-Dame-de-l'Osier. Pamphlet.

Revista Guadalupe, Conozca Toda la Historia de una Advocacion Universal. The Shrine of Our Lady of Guadalupe. Estremadura, Spain. 1983.

Sharkey, Don and Joseph Debergh, O.M.I. *Our Lady of Beauraing.* Hanover House. Garden City, New York. 1958.

Swann, Ingo. *The Great Apparitions of Mary.* The Crossroad Publishing Company. New York. 1996.

Walsh, William J. *The Apparitions and Shrines of Heaven's Bright Queen.* v. 3. 1906.

ABOUT THE AUTHOR

Joan Carroll Cruz is a native of New Orleans who relocated to Ponchatoula, Louisiana as a result of the Katrina flooding. She is the educational product of the School Sisters of Notre Dame. She attended grade school, high school and college under their tutelage. About her teachers Mrs. Cruz says, "I am especially indebted to the sisters who taught me for five years at the boarding school of St. Mary of the Pines in Chatawa, Mississippi. I cannot thank them enough for their dedication, their fine example and their religious fervor which made such an impression on me."

Mrs. Cruz has been a tertiary in the Discalced Carmelite Secular Order (Third Order) for many years. She is married to Louis Cruz, the retired owner of a swimming pool repair and maintenance business. They are the proud parents of five children.

Mrs. Cruz's books include: *The Incorruptibles*; *Eucharistic Miracles*; *Mysteries, Marvels, and Miracles*; *Saints for the Sick*; *Secular Saints*, and others that were published by TAN Books.